Praise for
YOU'LL GROW OUT OF IT

"A book like Jessi Klein's YOU'LL GROW OUT OF IT comes along to remind us just what an artful confessional essay can do."

—*New York Times*

"Is it really a surprise that comedian Jessi Klein, head writer and executive producer for *Inside Amy Schumer*, would write a book of personal essays brimming with sharp observations and insights and poignant recollections but that above all is very, very funny?...We guarantee that this book will quickly become one of your summer favorites."   —*Entertainment Weekly*

"[Jessi Klein's] astute, hilarious essays about the perilous path to modern womanhood will have you wincing in recognition."   —*People*

"Chances are Jessi Klein made you ugly-laugh...laugh even harder with the comedian's essay collection."

—*Marie Claire*

"Her arguments are sharp, her confessions just light enough, and—most crucially—her quips LOL-worthy on almost every page."   —*Vulture*

"Klein should be considered a frontrunner to fill the void left behind by the late essayist Nora Ephron."

—Metro Canada

"A sharp, witty collection of essays that will make you say, 'Same, TBH.'"

—*Flare*

"A must-read for former (and current) tomboys everywhere."

—Romper.com

"[Jessi Klein] is so casually open at the most illuminating moments in her book that you feel you're sitting with a friend, wineglass in hand, picking up where you left off the Friday night before. It's the tagline of just about every female comic's memoir, but it rings especially true with Klein."

—*The National Post*

"An excellent showcase for her self-deprecating, transgressive humor."

—*Toronto Star*

"Both smart and absurd, Klein's essays are written with a David Sedaris–like affinity for language."

—*Winnipeg Free Press*

"Never afraid to share insights and reveal the raw truth behind her own stories, Klein makes readers laugh while inspiring them, a feat that calls to mind the work of the late Nora Ephron. This uplifting and uproarious collection of personal essays will be repeatedly shared among friends."   —*Publishers Weekly* (starred review)

"Reading [Jessi Klein's] book is like watching her—doubtless superb—stand-up act."
                                        —*Booklist* (starred review)

"A gifted comedian turns the anxieties, obsessions, insecurities, and impossible-to-meet expectations that make up human nature into laughter."
                                        —*Kirkus* (starred review)

You'll Grow Out of It

Jessi Klein

GRAND CENTRAL
PUBLISHING

NEW YORK   BOSTON

Copyright © 2016 by Jessi Klein
Cover design by Jennifer Carrow. Cover illustration © Kendra Dandy. Cover copyright ©
2017 by Hachette Book Group, Inc.

Grand Central Publishing
Hachette Book Group
1290 Avenue of the Americas, New York, NY 10104
grandcentralpublishing.com
twitter.com/grandcentralpub

Originally published in hardcover and ebook by Grand Central Publishing in July 2016.
First Trade Paperback Edition: July 2017

Grand Central Publishing is a division of Hachette Book Group, Inc. The Grand Central
Publishing name and logo is a trademark of Hachette Book Group, Inc.

The publisher is not responsible for websites (or their content) that are not owned by the
publisher.

The Hachette Speakers Bureau provides a wide range of authors for speaking events. To
find out more, go to www.hachettespeakersbureau.com or call (866) 376-6591.

Library of Congress Cataloging-in-Publication Data

Names: Klein, Jessi, 1975-
Title: You'll grow out of it / Jessi Klein.
Description: First edition. | New York : Grand Central Publishing, 2016.
Identifiers: LCCN 2016009270| ISBN 9781455531189 (hardback) | ISBN
9781478936619 (audio cd) | ISBN 9781478983798 (audio download) | ISBN
9781455531196 (ebook)
Subjects: LCSH: Klein, Jessi, 1975- | Women comedians—United
States—Biography. | BISAC: BIOGRAPHY & AUTOBIOGRAPHY / Entertainment
&
Performing Arts. | BIOGRAPHY & AUTOBIOGRAPHY / Women. | HUMOR /
Form /
Essays.
Classification: LCC PN2287.K6725 A3 2016 | DDC 792.702/8092 [B] —dc23 LC
record
available at https://lccn.loc.gov/2016009270

ISBNs: 978-1-4555-3120-2 (trade pbk.), 978-1-4555-3119-6 (ebook)

Printed in the United States of America

LSC-C

10 9 8 7 6 5 4 3

For Mom & Da & Michael & Asher

Contents

Tom Man   *1*

The Bath   *8*

Walking Through the Cloud   *14*

Dale   *19*

How to Get Older   *27*

All the Cakes   *37*

Bar Method and the Secrets of Beautiful Women   *45*

Poodle vs. Wolf   *54*

The Cad   *63*

Anthropologie   *86*

Types   *92*

The Bachelor   *98*

Connie   *106*

Carole King and the Saddest To-Do List Ever   *116*

The Lingerie Dilemma   124

How to Get Engaged   139

The Wedding Dress   156

Long Day's Journey into Porn   172

Leap of Faith   187

Ma'am   202

How I Became a Comedian   209

Dogshit   234

Get the Epidural   250

The Infertility Chapters   261

Acknowledgments   289

Tom Man

Everyone is charmed by a little tomboy. A scrappy little girl in overalls with a ponytail and scraped knees, who loves soccer and baseball and comic books and dirt. But what are we charmed by? It's not just that she's cute. It's that she so innocently thinks she's going to stay this way forever. But we all know she won't. And why is that?

Because as much as we like a tomboy, nobody likes a tom man.

You might be wondering, "What is a tom man? I've never heard this term before." You are correct. That is because I invented it. It is the only thing I have ever invented.

A tom man is what happens when a tomboy just never grows out of it.

For as far back as I can remember, the voice in my head has sounded like the voice of a man. You might think the next thing I'm going to tell you has something to do with being gay, or thinking I'm a man trapped in a woman's body, but neither is the case. What I mean is that literally, walking around as a child, the little voice I'd hear narrating my own thoughts and experiences sounded like Daniel Stern in *The Wonder Years*. I think this is because the very idea of possessing an "inner voice" felt by definition like a male characteristic. In contrast, the tent poles of "femininity" as I observed them—high heels, eye makeup, Diet Coke, smiling, etc.—all seemed to be focused on the external. In any case, they felt completely foreign to me.

As a result, throughout my childhood, I felt like an outsider to being a straight girl, even though I WAS a straight girl.

My parents, perhaps noticing that my main recreational activity was counting the yellow cabs that went past our window, asked if I wanted to do ballet. I said absolutely not, as the idea of wearing a tutu repulsed me. I have a very early memory of viscerally hating, loathing, a girl in my preschool, simply because she wore earrings. The overt femininity of this act was somehow an irritant to me. Even though I was just four years old, I remember having the "What do you think, you're bettah than me?" feeling that a fifty-year-old plumber from Brooklyn feels when he has to take a detour because Prince William is in town.

To punish her I would ram my Big Wheel into her Big Wheel until she cried.

My only nod to typical girl interests was that I loved

horses and devoured every book in the *Black Stallion* series, and when I was finished with those books I would
stare at the covers, taking in how beautiful horses were in
general and the Black Stallion was in particular. Lots of
people talk about the sexual undertones of girls' interest
in horses, but I know that for me, when I stared at those
pictures, I didn't have some secret desire to date the Black
Stallion. I literally wanted to be a horse. A male horse.

But it's still acceptable to be a tomboy through elementary school. And even into the beginning of junior high, a
girl who dresses or acts more like a boy can be filed under
"coltish," the adjective for the next age category. But I was
pushing it. I didn't regularly brush my hair.[1] I didn't have
any interest in makeup beyond the moment that I stole a
pink frosted Wet n Wild lipstick in the fourth grade just
because my friend Mara did.[2] In the sixth grade, I was allowed for the first time to eat lunch outside the confines
of the school, and with this newfound culinary freedom I
chose to eat a single street-cart hot dog every single day.

Once I reached high school, however, my transfor-
mation from Pippi Longstocking–esque tomboy to are-
you-a-lesbian-or-what tom man began in earnest. I was
supposed to be entering into the full bloom of puberty,

---

1 This led to an epic impromptu comb-out by my friend's little sister
 Gracie one Sunday afternoon. As it turns out, I had a matted hairball the
 size of a pregnant hamster living at the nape of my neck.
2 I learned later, to my complete horror, that my mother has held on to this
 lipstick and has been using it for *decades*. This kind of unself-consciously
 gross behavior, of course, was part of what my tom manhood was mod-
 eled upon.

nibbling, like a delicate baby panda, at the first tiny bamboo shoots of womanhood. But I resisted. Even though I was interested in men, and wanted a boyfriend desperately, I didn't relate to any of the activities women partake in to create the circumstances where a teenage boy might be coaxed into the role. I wore my dad's old button-down cowboy shirts with enormous shapeless jeans and combat boots. I have a memory of walking home from school one afternoon when a homeless man hanging out on the corner of my block felt compelled to inquire whether I was "a man or a woman."

I looked like a mess during college, too, although I did manage at one point to get a decent little bob haircut (for free on a training night from Vidal Sassoon). While the girls around me were starting to exercise, hunching over a StairMaster in that way that people did in the '90s, sensing, as they should have, that now was the time to start laying a foundation upon which firm booties and high tits would remain forever tightly slung, I wasn't aware that any such activity was necessary. And it didn't ever occur to me to eat anything other than breaded chicken patties on Wonder Bread buns followed by a piece of cake. I've thought about it pretty hard, and I feel certain that I ate at least one of those chicken patties every single day for the full four years I was at school.

Somehow, in the midst of this, I did manage to wrangle up a boyfriend, but that didn't stop me from being a tom man. Even though he was, in fact, an actual man, he suffered from the same late-bloomer syndrome I did, wherein neither of us knew how to be a presentable adult. So essentially we ended up enabling each other, like drug addicts, except the only thing we were addicted to was looking terrible. When we moved in together after college, into a tired junior one-bedroom, we put our mattress on the floor, sleeping together like a couple of Labradors, blinking away the dust bunnies that cold breezes would blow into our faces. Even when I started working in an office, sartorially I still looked more than a smidge like a rodeo clown. I remember buying a pair of wide-legged parachute-material pants in gunmetal gray, and wearing those with bright-orange Adidas sneakers and a button-down short-sleeved blouse I got on sale from Banana Republic for $29.99. All my shirts, throughout my entire twenties, cost $29.99.

And perhaps because my boyfriend was also desperately inexperienced, and thus had very few demands, I didn't feel the need to participate in any of the seductive arts. I wore Hanes Her Way underwear every single day, no exceptions. Because they were the "bikini" kind I felt like pretty hot shit, but make no mistake, for me "her way" meant plain white cotton with a little bit of pubic hair sticking out the sides.

Once he and I broke up, I suddenly found myself single, with the predicament of having to get naked in front of new men. I felt lost, like a monkey born in captivity that, despite a researcher's attempt to release it back into the wild, cowers in the corner of its cage, desperate for its safe old life.

I was still essentially feral, and beyond shaving my legs above the knee, I made few noticeable external changes. But for the first time, I started dating guys who gave me unsolicited feedback on my appearance.

I remember I was once resting my legs on a boyfriend's lap as we lolled about on the couch. He looked down at my toenails and said, "So you never use nail polish, huh?" I stared down at my feet. My toenails were bare and, truth be told, the ends were a little ragged. They were the toenails of someone who had just scaled a cliff, except I hadn't scaled anything (ever). I felt a pang of primal shame, the female grooming equivalent of Eve suddenly losing her innocence upon realizing that she was naked, like a total idiot.

Then there was the night I arrived at a bar to meet my old friend Kate. Kate is a guy's gal, but she is not a tom man. She's more of a Katharine Hepburn–style broad, a ball-busting pants wearer who is still very feminine. I was arriving straight from work, which meant I was carrying my huge maroon backpack, overflowing with papers and books and loose change and probably a CD Walkman. After giving her a hug, I lowered my backpack onto the floor. Kate stared at it for a moment, as if it were a puppy that had just shit on a white rug, and then leaned in toward me and put her hand on my knee.

"Jess, you know I love you," she said, "but your backpack is hurting my feelings."

I was taken aback. This wasn't a boyfriend telling me that he thought my butt looked big in a skirt. This was a friend, an amiga, a woman with no investment in my appearance beyond platonic affection. And still, she felt it necessary to inform me that I had crossed a line.

At the time of the backpack incident, I was probably around thirty, and like my little-girl tomboy self I had nontraditional interests. I was doing stand-up comedy, which meant that I was hanging out in dive bars and telling jokes to strangers. I was proud that I had finally gathered up the guts to pursue this weird calling that I'd felt I had since I was a ten-year-old girl dressed as Groucho Marx for Halloween.

But dressing like Groucho for Halloween when you're ten is different from dressing like Groucho as a consistent style choice when you're thirty. I was single and living by myself in a dark sublet across from the BQE in Brooklyn and I wanted to get out of there. I was sick of dating funny but emotionally stunted guys. I wanted to find a Grown Man. It seemed only fair, I decided, that if that was what I wanted, then I should make some attempt to become a Grown Woman. But when I looked at what it would mean to become a woman—one of those standard grown-up ladies, like the ones from commercials for gum or soda or shampoo—it all seemed to involve shrinking rather than growing.

The Bath

There are only a few commercials from my childhood that remain vivid in my memory. Some of them are imprinted because they were selling products I wanted very badly. At the top of my list was the Snoopy Sno-Cone Machine, a plastic doghouse in which you stuffed ice in the door and poured syrup into the chimney, then turned a handle a few times, and voilà, you got a sno-cone. I still remember the exact notes of the jingle and how this toy seemed to combine everything I wanted—sugar, cold, Snoopy, something we couldn't afford. Other ads I remember because despite the fact that they ran constantly, I was too young to figure out what they were really selling. Of these, the one I recall most vividly is that famous spot for Calgon, in which a beautiful woman who's seriously about to lose her shit tells us about everything that is making life unmanageable: "The traffic! [Shot of apocalyptic 1970s traffic.] The boss! [Shot of cliché mustachioed rapey boss yelling into a telephone.] The baby! [Shot of cliché baby crying.] THE

DOG! [Shot of an adorable sheepdog who doesn't appear to have done anything wrong, but whose existence has pushed her over the edge for some reason.] That does it!" she declares, submitting to her nervous breakdown. "Calgon, TAKE ME AWAY!"

They would then cut to her in an enormous circular tub overflowing with bubbles. The set was in some kind of pseudo-Greco-Roman columned whitespace, but it had the same remote feeling as the sets on *Star Trek*—as if she'd totally left earth behind. Even the word *Calgon* itself seemed galactically foreign, like *Argo*. But wherever she was, she was happy. "I LOVE IT," she reported from the spacetub, finally relaxed.

Despite watching this spot literally hundreds of times, I was never clear on exactly what product I was being sold. Was it the tub itself? If it was simply a bubble bath, what would be its relationship to the dog and the boss and the baby and the traffic?

Looking back, I realize the reason I was so confused was because I didn't get the notion of a bath as something transporting, as an escape from the overwhelming pressure of the average female life. To me a bath was just a bath, and I never particularly liked taking baths. Calgon was selling the bath as a solution to a problem I was too young to understand.

Then I grew up.

I now understand that there is a whole cottage industry around bathing. And though it existed before Oprah, Oprah blew that shit way up. For years, she has championed the notion of bathing as the ultimate luxury, the place and experience where she is her happiest. Given how much she talks about it, I am fairly certain she spends more time in water than on dry land. Just recently in *O* magazine, the magazine for people who love O(prah), she wrote an article about "letting go of things" in which she admitted that her most prized possession on earth was a bathtub she had had custom-made for her, hand-carved from (she repeats this over and over) a single piece of Italian onyx. She writes, "Those of you who regularly read this column know that bathing is my hobby.[1] I revel in all things that enhance the experience, which is why, over the years, you've seen so many bath products on 'The O List'…they delight my senses and help soothe me, body and soul."

OKAY OPRAH WE GOT IT.

It seems like most women agree with Oprah. They love to take baths. But I never liked to and still don't. Besides Calgon, there are two other pop-culture images of women in the bath that come to my mind: One is Julia Roberts in *Pretty Woman*, up to her neck in bubbles and rocking out to Prince, happy in the knowledge that soon Richard Gere will buy her out of prostitution! The other is of Glenn Close at the end of *Fatal Attraction*, seemingly drowned by Michael Douglas but then popping up one last time with a kitchen knife before getting shot in the chest and sinking back into the water. It's exciting but sad.

---

1 Oprah's hobby is BATHING.

I tend to think more about Glenn Close than Julia Roberts.

To me there has always been something vaguely miserable about bathing. The soaking, the sitting, the water getting dirty and cold, the inevitable random hair floating up against your skin, the pruning. It always makes me feel like I am stewing up the world's saddest soup out of myself. It hurts my neck. (I've thought about getting an inflatable bath pillow from Bed Bath & Beyond, but every collection of online product reviews contains at least one written by some angry woman who has been deeply disappointed that the bath pillow subtracted from, rather than enhanced, her experience. This is a risk I cannot afford.) I get hot and thirsty in the bath and when I stand up I always feel like I'm going to pass out. Because I feel less clean than when I got in, I have to take a shower afterward. Ultimately, it feels like I've gone backward, hygiene-wise.

But these are just my physical issues with the bath. My conceptual problems with bathing begin with the very same ideology some adman for Calgon decided to trade on forty years ago: the idea that the bath is the last space a woman can escape to, like a gazelle fleeing a lion by running into water up to her head. I feel like getting in the bath is a kind of surrender to the idea that we can't really make it on land, that we've lost the fight for a bedroom corner or even just our own chair in the living room. And once the bath becomes our last resort, a Stockholm syndrome occurs. We cede all other space to the husbands or boyfriends or kids and then convince ourselves that this is awesome! Yay, I'm submerged in a watery trough! This is incredible! This is my happy place! I definitely wouldn't prefer to just be lying in my own bed watching *Bachelor in Paradise*! I would much rather have grainy bath crystals imprinting into my butt than be in my own room! This is PERFECT!

I realize I'm being harsh here. And judgey. I know I know I know. It's just there's something so sad-lady about the bath to me, so Cathy cartoon. And I'm probably going overboard. But there is one more important point to consider:

Men don't take baths. There are exceptions, of course, but like all exceptions they prove the rule. I know they don't take baths because I have never known a man who likes to take baths except in cases of extreme medicinal need. Also, I went on Facebook and conducted a very scientific poll, asking hundreds of friends if any of the men, or the men that the women know, take baths. And the answer, almost across the board, was no. Some men wrote of hating them and finding them disgusting, and moreover being completely bewildered by women's fascination with them.

I asked my husband, Mike, why he thinks women are so obsessed with baths.

"Maybe because women like to smell good? Women care about smelling good. Or because they get to use products? Women like products. Oh, or—maybe because they get to be weightless!"

(The weightlessness was something I hadn't considered. I remember going to the Hayden Planetarium a few years ago and finding an area where you could stand on different scales to see what you would weigh on other planets. One woman was getting on a scale to weigh herself on the moon and she handed her purse to her friend. SHE HANDED HER PURSE TO HER FRIEND so that she wouldn't THROW OFF HER WEIGHT ON THE MOON.)

Men do not care about being weightless. But I think there is a bigger reason that they hate to bathe as much as women love it.

I think it's because they sense what I know: that the bath is where you go when you've run out of options.

I worry that one day I will be a mother who ends up in the bath, reading a water-crinkled old book that I've been trying to finish for over a year, squeezing the last gloops of peppermint something or other from a plastic bottle into the water, wishing that there was more space for me than this.

This is why Virginia Woolf stressed the importance of having a room of one's own. If you don't fight for it, don't insist on it, and don't sacrifice for it, you might end up in that increasingly tepid water, pruning and sweating while you dream of other things.

Walking Through the Cloud

In the last few years, I've been learning the secrets of being a woman. Maybe you didn't even know there were secrets. I never used to think there were any, either, but that's just because I didn't know them.

Sorry to digress. What do I mean by secrets? Why is there a secret to being a woman at all? Being a woman usually means you are born with a vagina and after that you'll probably grow boobs and most likely pretty soon after that you'll have long hair because it's no secret that men are pretty non-negotiable about that, except for the times when some Frenchwoman with an insanely long neck pulls it off and a certain segment of men who are open to being a little different go fucking bananas for her. Honorable mention to Tilda Swinton, who is doing her own thing in that area, and I believe that not only does she know the secrets to being a woman, she knows the secret to being immortal. You watch. We will all die before she does.

I got distracted again. The topic is: What do I mean by secrets?

Well, the beginning:

When I was five, my mother taught me my first secret. But I should just say here that my mom was not a traditionally feminine woman. I mean, she's a woman, and she's feminine, but she has simply never cared about almost any of the bullshit you need to do to have the world look at you. And it's not hard to understand why, when you consider the fact that she had three kids in a two-bedroom apartment with no dishwasher and no microwave and was much busier clipping coupons and carrying a laundry bag up and down six flights of stairs. She is naturally beautiful, but I don't think that's why she didn't wear makeup. She always claimed that she didn't know how to put it on. She has still never had a manicure or pedicure, and we never had conditioner in the house, just a cheap shampoo called Fermo Caresse.

However:

My mom always wore a scent. In the 1970s and '80s it came mainly from oils in little golden vials that she'd buy off a fold-up table from an African man in a dashiki on the subway platform. But at some point she came into a real-life spray perfume. She must not have spent much money on it, or maybe it was a gift, but in either case we were both transfixed by the bottle, a golden rectangle with hard glass edges that refracted the light. Unlike the budget oil-in-vials that you'd have to just kind of smudge onto yourself, this perfume had a button on it that you'd depress with your index finger, which would create a beautiful fancy rich-lady cloud.

My instinct was to put the bottle one inch from my face and then keep spraying until it was empty and ready to go in the garbage. But one afternoon my mother saw me getting started on this project and told me she wanted to show me something. I remember it was afternoon because I can see that specifically brownish 1980s New York light coming through the window, pressing through the cartoony leaf embroidery of the curtains in the cramped little bedroom I shared with my sister, every inch of which was crammed with our great-grandmother's old furniture: a dresser with a mirror, a rocking chair.

"That's not how you do it," she said, gently prying the perfume bottle from my hands. We moved to the kitchen, the largest room in the apartment, a room with a couple of feet of floor space.

"You have to walk through the cloud," she said.

"What?" I asked.

"Like this," she said, and she reached her hand to a full arm's length from her body, pumped out one small puff of fancy-lady cloud spray, and then quickly, but delicately, light on her toes, walked through the droplets. It was a round trip. She walked four paces, then did a perfect pivot and walked back.

"That's how you put on perfume," she said. "You walk through the cloud. The scent is more subtle. You don't want to reek."

She handed me the bottle to try. I pushed the button out in front of me and made a small cloud. I ran through it and back, like I was jumping through a sprinkler. I could feel a little of the perfume's coolness on my face and even a slight burning of the alcohol in my nose. When I was done, I sniffed my sleeve and inhaled the whisper of a smell that had settled like dew on my shirt.

My mother was right: I didn't want to reek. I wanted to be like her. She smelled amazing. And I was fascinated by this ritual, as ridiculous as it looked. I loved that it was something my dad didn't know to do. I felt like I'd been inducted into a secret society. Women walk through clouds.

But that was pretty much it for the secrets that my mom taught me. The others I started to pick up as I moved through the world with increasing independence. I learned about those little teal boxes of bleach you can buy at the drugstore that hide your mustache (they don't). I learned about taking the pill at the same time every day and about never leaving your drink unattended.

But maybe the most important lesson I learned was when I was just eight and I walked in on my twelve-year-old brother and his friend gawking at a magazine and laughing. Curious to know what they were looking at, I made myself as annoying as possible until my brother's friend shrugged and handed me a *Hustler* open to a picture of a woman with her legs spread apart. Her skin was a tawny orange, basically the color of a new football. But mainly I remember being shocked to see that between her legs was something pink and raw, something that I was 100 percent certain was not a body part I possessed. I felt the beginning of a fear that there was something horribly wrong with me.

This was when I learned one of the biggest secrets of being a woman, which is that much of the time, we don't feel like we're women at all.

Dale

The morning of my twenty-eighth birthday I woke up at the happiest place on earth, aka the Enchanted Kingdom, aka Disney World, aka why the hell am I here? Actually, I was there for the wedding of my little sister, who, in a kind of *Sixteen Candles* twist, had decided she was going to get married at Disney World on the day before my birthday. Just to be clear, it wasn't like she and her fiancé were "getting married at Disney World" because they wanted to be ironic and hilarious. We weren't wearing Von Dutch trucker caps and drinking PBR. It was more like she and her fiancé were wholeheartedly, super fucking into Disney World and were mega-psyched to get married there.

Now, my family is Jewish, and my sister's fiancé was a Conservative Jew, so when my sister told us they wanted to get married at Disney World, we were collectively very surprised and collectively very not stoked. I decided to try to talk some sense into her, and the talk went basically like this:

"You know that people say Walt Disney was a Nazi sympathizer, right? Mauschwitz, haha?"

But my sister, who is very rational-minded, is all, "That's not true."

And I'm all, "Right, I know, but like—you know what I mean."[1]

But she wasn't having it and went forward with the Disney plan.

So the icing on the cake is that my sister casually mentions to me one day that she and her fiancé have decided to pay extra in order to have the Disney "characters" attend the reception. At which point I just decide that if I am single, and I'm going to be at Disney World the weekend of my birthday, then I am definitely going to try to get laid, and if I can at all swing it I am definitely fucking one of the characters. In my mind I put my hopes on Tigger, who, I won't lie to you, I've always found very attractive. I've always admired his barrel chest and his upbeat approach to life.

So my plan is to depart on Friday morning for the rehearsal dinner, which is Friday night. Because I leave everything till the last minute, I wait until Thursday morning to pick up my bridesmaid dress, which is an ornately embroidered floor-length number in a body-hugging, light-reflective lavender sateen. At around

---

1   I don't actually know if there's proof that Walt Disney hated Jews, but…you know what I mean.

four thirty that afternoon, just as I'm wrapping up a long workday of personal emailing and Googling myself, all the lights and my computer pop off, as the Northeast is plunged into the worst blackout in the history of the United States. With the subway shut down, I join the throng of humanity trudging home in the mind-blowing August heat from Midtown to Brooklyn. However, I do notice that I am the only one in the throng with a thirty-pound purple bridesmaid dress slung over my shoulder.

With all power in the city still out, I come dangerously close to not making it to the wedding. In fact, I don't make it to the rehearsal dinner. When I arrive at the Delta terminal, I find out that not only do they have no power, but miraculously, in a post-9/11 world, they have absolutely no plan for dealing with having no power—no emergency generator, no nothing. Due to the lack of power, they won't let anyone into the terminal, but they also won't say for sure if any planes will be taking off that day. A guy with a megaphone literally tells us it's a "crapshoot," which is never a word you want to hear when it comes to anything regarding air travel. Me and about three hundred other people end up baking on the sidewalk for about seven hours while pretty much dehydrating because there is no food or water anywhere. I am lucky enough to have a small amount of peach Snapple backwash that I guard as if it's gold bullion.

Ultimately, no Delta planes leave that day, and I am

only able to get a ticket for the next morning—it is the last one left on any carrier from New York to Orlando, and it's a one-way from Continental for the not-so-reasonable price of $800. Nevertheless, I must pay it. It's my sister's wedding. It's Disney.

Because I am so stressed out, right before I get on the flight I decide to take an Ambien, forgetting that you really should not take a whole ten-milligram Ambien before a two-hour flight. I make it to the Kingdom just minutes before the wedding is scheduled to begin, and I'm completely hallucinating. Upon my arrival to the Enchanted Castle, the wedding planner greets me by screaming, "GO DIRECTLY TO HAIR!!! GO DIRECTLY TO HAIR!!!" I deliriously weave my way to hair.

The Ambien is only just wearing off at the beginning of the reception, by which time I'm so exhausted that I decide the only logical thing to do is get massively drunk while waiting for the characters to arrive. The fascinating thing about the way Disney does the characters' entrances is that, in terms of celebrity, they go B list, then C list, then A list—so first Donald and Daisy come in, then the chipmunk cousins Chip and Dale, and just when you can't stand the wait a minute longer, because you're dying to see them and you're just going to burst if you don't see them right away, Minnie and Mickey finally make a grand entrance and everyone loses their shit.

So they start us doing the hora—because it is a Jewish wedding, after all—and the character whose hand I end up holding is Dale, and fairly quickly we begin what I can only describe as a passionate flirtation. First we're just dancing together. After a while we're slow dancing, my torso pressed against his furry underbelly. I think a large part of the sensuality of the experience is that the characters aren't allowed to speak at all; they're totally silent. Also, you can't see into their eyes, which are just black pits of vast, endless nothing.

Hours go by and I'm completely wasted but totally happy. We're entwined on the dance floor, the envy of all the other interspecies couples in the room. I have my head on his shoulder, "Lady in Red" is playing, and I decide there will never be a more perfect moment to make my move. I squeeze his paw, look up at him, and whisper as seductively as one can after two vodka tonics and four glasses of (Disney) Chardonnay, "Hey—do you want to come back to my room? I'm staying at the Contemporary Resort in room 2629." Dale steps back. He looks at me solemnly—or maybe happily, it's hard to tell—and chirps, "Chchchchch!"

That's it. It's clear to me that if he were to attempt to consummate our passion, he would be fired, and possibly killed. We part ways and I go back to my room alone. I am sad that my soul mate and I met at the wrong time, doomed by the rules of a Draconian kingdom, until it occurs to me a week later that the person in the costume was not necessarily, and most likely wasn't, a man.

* * *

The next morning is my birthday. I am twenty-eight, alone, and lying on a twin-size bed with Eeyore sheets. And even though my flight doesn't leave till ten a.m., I decide to bail on Disney World at about six and just hang out at the airport because my room at the Contemporary Resort is so unbearably ugly that I can't be in there another minute. I guess it was "Contemporary" when it was built in 1971, but now all the décor is horribly outdated and garish—the wall mirror, for instance, is shaped kind of like an amoeba, because that is totally crazy and in the '70s people apparently liked everything totally CRAZY!

I hang out at the gate and watch the sun rise, until finally a woman comes to open up and start checking people in. Even though I never, ever, play the birthday card, I decide that because of the blackout horror, I'm going to allow it just this once to try to upgrade to first. And she's very kind, but apologizes and says there's no first class on the plane. However, she promises that they'll make sure to "take care of me." I don't totally know what that means, but I'm picturing an exit-row seat, extra blankets, maybe a little plastic glass of champers.

So an hour later about two hundred people are at the gate and everyone's cranky because the flight, once again, is delayed. At last the Delta woman gets on the loudspeaker and goes, "I want to thank y'all for choosing Delta Song today, and we should be able to board y'all in about an hour. But first, I think y'all should know we have a birthday girl with us today, her name is Jessi, so why don't we all sing 'Happy Birthday' to her!" Everyone at the gate starts singing "Happy Birthday" to me, and it's actually a really lovely, life-affirming moment. I can't help but think to myself, *You know what? You had a rough weekend, but people are basically good. They really are. We're all just on this crazy blue marble together.*

The plane finally takes off. Because this is Delta's new "Song" division, the one that is trying to compete with JetBlue,[2] the stewardesses are referred to as "talent," and they crack puns constantly. I do not have a plastic cup of champers, but I have purchased myself a drink called The Sunset Strip, which is a mix of vodka, mango, and orange juice. It is wonderful, and it is making the flight wonderful. Shortly after takeoff, one of the "talent" suddenly gets on the intercom and announces, "I want to thank you all for choosing Song today, please let us know if you need anything. I also want to point out that it seems we have a BIRTHDAY girl among us today, her name is Jessi and she's in seat 17C, why don't we all join in singing her 'Happy Birthday'!" Suddenly, everyone is looking at me like I'm the world's biggest jackass because I seem like the douchebag who needs to tell every single person I meet that it's my birthday, as if I'm five years old. All the other passengers are completely silent and freaked out because obviously the gate woman on the ground did not communicate with the "talent."

And then I hear one guy who's sitting eight or nine

---

2   Delta Song failed. It is no longer with us. This is not a surprise.

seats back bark really loud, "We already FUCKIN' sang it!" And that's when I slump down in my seat and remember that people are bad, they're mostly bad, and wait to get back to New York, where the lights are finally back on.

How to Get Older

I was having one of those moments where you're feeling a little insecure and you want to prompt your boyfriend to say something complimentary by asking a question to which he must surely know there is only one acceptable answer.

In fairness to me, I did not ask Mike if I looked fat. I'm not an amateur. I know that men hate that question and resent you for asking it. Asking a man if you look fat is a sure guarantee that he will look at you and see Gilbert Grape's mom.

What I asked him was, "Do you think I'm going to age well?"

He replied: "I know you're going to age well, because you're already aging well."

Oy.

I had just turned thirty-eight. And I was having a thing, for the first time in my life, where when I looked in the mirror, my face looked a little—I dunno—I didn't look bad per se; I just couldn't put my finger on it. I didn't look old. I would search and search for exactly what the problem was, and then one night, staring at the ceiling unable to sleep, I realized what it was.

I just didn't look young anymore.

And then this other thing happened:

I was at an industry party thrown by a network. I won't say which one but let's call it COX. Agents and executives in suits were mingling with comedians at a glorified sports bar. I was getting ready to leave when an executive at COX ran up to me and put her face right up to mine. "Jessi! Don't go! I'm obsessed with you!" She was just rounding third from medium drunk to very drunk.

"You need to live in LA!" she yelled.

"Why?" I yelled back.

"So that I can put you in one of our shows!" she insisted, grabbing both of my arms. The bar was dark, but I could see that her face, which wasn't unattractive, seemed to have some odd angles, like someone had brainstormed a few ideas about where her cheeks were supposed to be. It was impossible to tell her age, in that LA way where someone is either thirty-five or is dead and has been dead for years. I wanted to leave, but sadly, there was a part of me that was flattered someone from COX could see me on COX.

"What do you think I could play?" I asked her as I started thinking about how I would break it to Mike that we were moving to LA. I pictured us driving across the country listening to Joni Mitchell's "California" all the way.

She stepped back so she could really take me in. Her face lit up.

"You could play Natalie Portman's mom!"

!

‼

‼‼

At home, hiding under my bed, I Googled "Natalie Portman."

She is six years younger than me.

But this is what it is now, to be this age. In entertainment, if you are a day over thirty, you are seen as being a viable great-great-grandmother to Elle Fanning.

I actually had already lived in LA during my early thirties, and it was there, on an unfortunate makeup-buying excursion to Barneys with my friend Jessica, that I had my first personal experience with the revulsion that exists toward female aging. We were at the Chanel counter, where a nice woman swooped in to help Jessica find a red lipstick. This left me paired with a permanently annoyed man who looked like Nathan Lane's evil twin. "What are you looking for?" he asked curtly. I told him I was just in the market for a blush brush, and he gave me a look that let me know I may as well have told him to go fuck himself directly to hell.

"Can I speak freely?" he asked, taking a step back to look at this frumpled sea monster from New York. I hated him but I also felt like he was about to tell me the most important thing any human has ever said to another.

"Right now, your priority needs to be your undereye area."

I remember how he stressed that word. "Your *priority*." Forget paying your rent and maintaining your relationships. Put off charity work and don't worry about voting in the general election because your PRIORITY right now needs to be your UNDEREYE AREA. I had never really thought about my undereye area before, but the truth is in the days leading up to my Barneys outing my undereye area had been something of a mess. Dry, flaking, red. Evil Nathan Lane wasn't making this up.

For $150, I bought a thingy of Chanel eye cream about the circumference of a bottle cap. Nevertheless, despite my making my undereye area a priority, over the next few weeks it proceeded to get worse. I finally went to a dermatologist who told me I was having a severe eczema reaction to the wildfires that were burning all around the Valley. In recent weeks, the air over LA had been purple with ash. She said applying any product on top of the irritation was probably making it worse. So basically, the Chanel counter guy had assumed that it was my disgusting decaying female face that was my eye problem, not the fact that the FUCKING CITY WAS ON FIRE.

Still. I was no longer an innocent to the knowledge that I had arrived at the age where I was supposed to be buying premium $kin products. I read enough magazines to know that celebrity ladies are not fucking around in aisle three of Duane Reade (Rite Aid in LA). Any number of fancy famous women may be spokeswomaning for Revlon, but in reality that is probably what they are slathering on their dogs. They use the expensive stuff.

And mainly, they use La Mer. La Mer is to famous actresses over thirty what Gatorade is to athletes. The mythology around La Mer is that it comes from seaweed found at the bottom of the deepest ocean and was originally developed as a treatment for burn patients. Realizing that every woman is essentially a burn patient (insofar as our faces are constantly being scorched by the raging fire of time), some brilliant scientist smeared it all over a lady's skin and now the smallest container of it costs $265. There is no more disgusting secret about my life than the fact that in the last few years I have bought into the idea that I need La Mer/am worth it. And now I buy a couple of jars a year. This despite the fact that I used to listen to Nirvana and Hole and still have trouble buying socks that don't come in a bag because I just can't believe a single pair costs more than six bucks.

It is hard not to look to celebrities for confirmation that you can be old and still be a sexy woman. The bummer is that there are only about four such women in Hollywood who are seen this way, the chief example being Susan Sarandon. She's been carrying the burden of being the hot "old" chick for about two decades now. It's admirable, and I would absolutely have sex with her, but I feel like the pressure on both of us at this point is getting a bit intense. It's hard to source all your emotional assurances about aging on the shoulders of just one especially bangable sixty-nine-year-old.

And the magazines, the magazines. I don't know why I read them and I feel guilty about it, but there's nothing

I can do, I want to look at the pictures even though they sometimes make me feel so bad about my stupid normal human appearance that my soul actually aches. Each of the fashion magazines—*Bazaar*, *Vogue*, *Elle*—does an annual issue called "Beautiful at Every Age" where their teams of editors really sweat it out to let their readers know that you can look and dress hot no matter how old you are. They dedicate various sections to women in their twenties, thirties, forties, fifties, sixties, and seventies, but there are two decimating things going on here:

1. The models for every age category are always teenagers. For example, in the section for what sixty-year-old women can wear to look attractive, they'll say, "Oh, you'd look amazing in a suede cape and a sailor shirt," but the editorial photo is always of a teenage girl who looks like a fawn that is in its first minute of standing on its legs, essentially sending the message, "Here is how you can look beautiful in your sixties but we're not totally sure it will work and maybe you'll still look like a hag and we're scared we've made a mistake so just in case here's a photo of a nubile child and just use your imagination about the old part."

2. The other terrifying thing is that no magazine ever offers any vision of beauty beyond the "seventies" section, even though shit tons of women are living well past that. So if you happen to have made it to eighty or beyond, according to Anna

Wintour, you have fallen off the outermost edges of the attractiveness map into an old invisible sea where not even the wrinkle-erasing kelp of La Mer on the ocean floor will save your drooping shar-pei face.

And so here I am at thirty-eight, staring into the mirror. And even though I do not look young anymore, I am now less concerned about my face (or, as Nora Ephron warned, my neck) than I am about my newest problem area, my hands. In the last two years, my hands have taken on a decidedly gnarled affect. I'm not sure how or when my knuckles got thicker, but now my hands look like wizard hands, like they should be clutching a crystal ball. And my fingers, always long and a tad askew, seem to have become even more crooked, like the branch fingers on a wise old tree in an animated children's movie, who occasionally beckons to little kids and dispenses nuggets of truth like "Just be yourself, Toby." The tree is voiced by Morgan Freeman.

The thing is, taken part by part, I can handle my knotty paws and my sunken undereyes and all the little wilting tea leaves that foretell my future unprettiness. My only real desire now is to create a plan as to what type of old woman I can successfully become. I've been staring at old ladies for quite some time now, and from what I've observed, there seem to be only three paths that allow you to retain some aspect of appeal that will keep people interested in you:

PATH ONE—YOU WERE A SUPERMODEL AND YOU ARE STILL A SUPERMODEL

This is clearly the best path. If you were born looking like Christy Turlington, you will continue to look like Christy Turlington into your nineties even if people have to squint a little to still see her in there. Sophia Loren still looks like a goddess because she was already a goddess. But what if you're not already a goddess? See Path Two—

PATH TWO—YOU ARE RICH

This is a very common path if you live on the Upper East Side of New York, or on a yacht that never docks for tax purposes. There are legions of women whose old-lady style is based on wearing their money. I have to say, in certain respects, it works. Maybe you are no longer twenty-one with perky little boobs, but you are wearing an Hermès watch and an Alexander Wang tunic shirt and Chloé flats and a sapphire necklace still wet from the *Titanic*. The twenty-one-year-old with perky boobs can't afford even one of these items. So in that respect, you have more power than her. Even if people don't want to fuck you anymore, no one is fucking with you. Because you have so much money. But what if you don't have this money? Please skip to Path Three—

PATH THREE—YOU'RE AN ECCENTRIC

This is the last option. And it will be my option. We see these women all the time. They're not leaning on beauty, and they're not leaning on money. They're leaning on character. They wear hot-pink tights and high-top sneakers. They wear big glasses and pillbox hats. They look like they might have once worked at *Interview* even though they didn't. Or they look like Betsey Johnson back in the 1980s, but now here in the present and much older. They're memorable and fun. They're kooky old ladies. When I see them, I feel a pulse of happiness that maybe I won't be so sad losing the little dollop of prettiness I was allotted. That maybe the secret to getting old and feeling okay is just buying an enormous silly hat and making people smile when they look at you because they think you're having a good time.

But maybe that's not what the hat is about. Maybe the real issue is not so much making other people think you're having a super-fun time creeping toward death; it's simply being seen. This is the lament of older women, and ultimately of all old people—that you become invisible. It is especially hard for women, though, whose entire lives have been spent spinning around the idea that if no one is staring at you, you've somehow failed. Maybe the silly hat is really a Hail Mary to get people to look at you, no matter the reason.

And maybe when you're at the age where *Vogue* can no

longer fathom how you could possibly dress yourself, it will all seem so incredibly ridiculous that you'll actually be in the mood for the hat. The most fuckit Kentucky Derby hat you can find.

I'm going to make the silly hat my priority.

All the Cakes

I have gone to therapy, texted all my best friends, and listened to a downloadable Buddhist lecture about forgiveness on my iPod, so I'm genuinely trying. But I still can't figure out whether to take my ex-boyfriend up on his offer of lunch.

"Let's catch up," the email says.

I am engaged, but seeing his name still tweaks me in my gut, which in turn makes me feel embarrassed. Why am I so weak that he still gets to me, more than ten years after we've broken up? The Buddhists say that you shouldn't let shame about pain cause you to feel a second, self-inflicted pain, which is good advice; but sometimes it's hard to do what the Buddhists say, mainly because so many of the people who currently talk about Buddhism are in those newfangled sweatpants with the cuffs on the ankles and are otherwise insufferable.

The last time we'd really spoken to each other was November 2001—three months after we'd officially broken up—when I screamed at him on a quiet block in Brooklyn Heights, outside what had been our shared home. The woman he was now dating stood next to him, aghast. A random passerby, a man, told me to be quiet. I yelled at him to fuck off. I punched Pete over and over again in the shoulder, because he deserved it. I also threw my makeup bag in the street. I'm less sure of why I did that. Whatever the reason, it was a bad idea, because the thing you forget as an adult having a tantrum is that unlike when you were two and having a tantrum, no one else is going to pick up the shit you throw on the ground. I watched my boyfriend's new girlfriend, the blonde in a houndstooth J.Crew coat, scurry to the safety of the opposite corner, possibly afraid for her life. She should have been. I was an angry monster who wanted to eat them both. I told him I would never forgive him, that he had lost me forever, and that I would never ever speak to him again.

So now I am deciding whether what I said that night will continue to be true.

Just before we'd discussed taking a break, I had started reading *What We Talk About When We Talk About Love*. I remember thinking maybe it wasn't the best idea to be delving into Raymond Carver when I was already feeling blue. Just looking at the paperback's cover, a Hopper-inspired illustration of a lady in the world's bleakest purple shirt sitting alone on the edge of a bed, was enough to make me pull the blankets over my head. Still, I'd been experiencing a growing sense of shame about my inability to read anything but *Us Weekly* since college, and I felt like I had to stick with it.

After Pete and I agreed that we needed time apart to "take a break," I decamped to my parents' place in Manhattan. The Carver book, along with most of my other possessions, stayed behind. I packed an atrocity of a red gym bag with whatever items of Gap clothing felt necessary at the time. As I rode the subway across the river, I felt certain I would be back soon. I was so very naive. I had never gone through a breakup before. I didn't know that genially agreeing to "take a break" is, in most cases, just the emotional amuse-bouche to having your heart shattered like a lightbulb being thrown under the wheel of a school bus. Which is, of course, what happened.

Three months later, post-shattering, my friend Kat agreed to drive me back to Brooklyn in her beat-up green car to pick up the rest of my stuff. The plan was: She would double-park and wait while I went up-stairs and quickly collected my possessions, such as they were: a Groucho Marx poster, my clothes, miscellaneous tchotchkes, and my books. I would then come down-stairs, we'd cram my stuff into the hatchback, drive back to my parents' house, order Thai food, and then she'd watch me cry in my childhood bedroom. It seemed like an airtight plan.

Pete and I weren't speaking, but he had emailed me to tell me he was going to be away for a few weeks. He was off in Europe, supposedly with a friend, but I'd heard through the grapevine that she was there too. It was a mystery to me how this person, this person who'd been my person for six years, had turned his feelings for me off like a faucet and was now, miraculously, tragically, fucking someone else. As I walked into our former shared home, it dawned on me that the place must be loaded with clues as to how this had occurred. Just as I stupidly thought romantic "breaks" led to happy reunions, I was also too young to know that purposely rifling through your ex's apartment to find the detritus of his sex life with his new girlfriend is one of the dumbest things you can do in this life. In two minutes, I would acquire that knowledge. But at the moment I walked in the door, I was still an innocent.

This is why I was determined to open every drawer, look in every pocket, and peek in every peekable corner of the apartment. One of the first places I decided to poke around was the refrigerator. Why was I looking in the refrigerator? I think because I wanted to know what he was eating without me.

I WANTED TO KNOW WHAT HE WAS EATING WITHOUT ME.

His birthday had been three days before. But that still didn't help me understand why there were no fewer than five cakes sitting in the fridge. I lifted the lids of their boxes. They were all really nice cakes. Some were half eaten, but a few had only one or two bites missing. And that's when a vision began to form in my head, of Pete and his new girlfriend holding hands at some twee Brooklyn bakery, laughing uproariously over the difficulty of deciding which birthday cake to buy. And then I imagined her saying, "Let's just get all the cakes!" because that's a manic pixie dream girl thing to say, and then the two of them carrying all these cakes home and taking a few bites of each, still laughing hysterically, before putting the cakes aside and having birthday sex. In my mind, this scene quickly went from being something I imagined might have happened to footage I was watching on a security camera.

I was certain this was the way it must have occurred. And with this certainty came an overwhelming physical desire to take the remainder of the five cakes and smear them all over his bed and bedroom walls.

I should say for the record that I am not a violent person, or even someone who particularly likes conflict. I have middle-child syndrome and generally bounce around rooms like a Labrador retriever trying to make sure everyone is okay. But in that moment, the desire to destroy was overwhelming. I wanted to leave frosting all over his sheets and pillowcases so that when he returned from vacation his bed would be teeming with roaches and maggots wiggling in every mattress coil. I wanted him to come home to a room that looked like a scene from *The Exorcist*.

I closed my eyes and was able to vividly picture how good it would feel, this release of fury and frosting. But some small part of me was also able to think about the aftermath; about how I would carry that action with me for the rest of my life and it would become some small but definite part of my DNA. About how it would be one of the maybe twenty decisions you make out of your whole life that truly changes something in you.

I would become someone who had smeared birthday cake all over her ex-boyfriend's bed.

For a long time, I stood perfectly still, with a cake in my hand, the surprising heft of it so tempting, trying to control myself, summoning powers of resistance. After about ten minutes, I took a deep breath, returned the cake, and walked away from the refrigerator.

The search continued, however. I went into the living room, where I went through his backpack and found a copy of a FedEx slip with her name and address on it. He had sent her a gift. Probably something quirky and charming, the kind of thing he used to give me. The kind of thing that led me to have a rubber mouse in a specific sweater pocket for years. The date on the slip indicated he had sent it months ago, while he and I had still been talking about trying to figure things out. The cakes called to me again, like sirens.

After fifteen minutes, the only thing left to search was the bedroom. I entered slowly, my heart pounding. Papers and clothes were strewn all over the floor. The bed itself was unmade, the sheets and blankets whirled into a spiral, like a NASA photo of a distant galaxy. It felt cosmically incomprehensible, the idea that Pete was sleeping with someone who wasn't me. This is why what I saw next was so genuinely shocking. You know how you read about people jogging on some nature path and then they see something weird sticking out of the bushes and it turns out to be a foot? That's what it's like to find another woman's ponytail holder beside your bed. It was there, next to a chewed-up piece of pink gum the size and shape of a cat's butthole.

When you see an unfamiliar hairband in your bedroom, it's like you can see your entire life getting small enough to fit into that little elastic loop, like the conclusion of an old-time movie where the final moment is slowly irised out by blackness until it disappears.

Shaking, I decided it was time to get out of there. I was gathering the last of my clothes into a garbage bag when something on the floor caught my eye. There, upside down on the rug, was my copy of *What We Talk About When We Talk About Love*. I reached to pick it up and felt something sticky and wet on my hand. I turned the book over and noticed some sort of clear goo spread across the picture of the sad lady in the purple shirt. I was confused until I noticed the culprit just a few inches away on the floor, small enough that I hadn't seen it when I walked in: a little bottle of Astroglide lubricant that had tipped over and oozed out onto my book.

My friends and I have debated the meaning of this. What we didn't debate, because it truly isn't debatable, is that finding your copy of Raymond Carver's *What We Talk About When We Talk About Love* covered in your ex-boyfriend's lube is a perfect poem of an image, a hateful little sonnet composed by the universe to memorialize the end of your relationship.

I'm still on the fence about lunch. But after years of reflection, I'm sure of one thing: I should have smeared the cakes.

Bar Method and the Secrets of Beautiful Women

When I was a teenager, I was so worried about my flat chest that I didn't think at all about my butt. Of all the mistakes I've made in my life, this may have been the stupidest. In fairness, it was the '80s, and boobs, like cocaine, reigned supreme. How was I to know that one day, coke would be replaced with molly, and boobs would be overshadowed by butts?

I didn't just neglect thinking about my butt; I was completely unaware that butts were on anyone's radar. In my head, God had put our butts in the back for a reason: mainly, because we weren't supposed to worry about them. Little did I know, our butts were in the back so men could talk about them without us knowing, until it was too late and we'd already spent our whole lives eating balls of mozzarella as if they were apples.

Large breasts were the goal, and when I had an unexpected Hail Mary boob growth spurt at the ripe old age of twenty-one, I relaxed; I believed I now had all the equipment I needed to be considered Desirable™. Unfortunately, the same year that I finally grew breasts (pretty good ones, too, if I can own that for a moment), *Out of Sight* was released, and Jennifer Lopez became a superstar. It was the cultural tipping point for butts. Oh, the irony. I suddenly realized that men would be, or—holy fuck—had been concerned about butts for years. I found myself turning around in front of a three-way mirror, really trying to see my own ass for the first time. It filled all three of the mirrors.

I have a softish, curvy, 1970s Jewish mom body. I'm in my late thirties (the very latest ones), and my butt is kind of a vague trapezoid. I know Gwyneth Paltrow has said her butt is her least favorite body part also, but I think we all know she is impossibly full of shit, even though I have both of her cookbooks and buy every magazine she's on the cover of and think of her all the time and sometimes think of her right before I go to sleep.

Nevertheless, I wasn't terribly concerned, because my boobs still seemed to work a kind of magic on men. Then I met Mike, and although I suppose you could say that overall I worked more magic on him than I've ever worked on anyone, since he actually wanted to marry me, I never felt that any of it was particularly boob-related. I never got the sense he was a boob guy. He just didn't seem as enthused about my breasts as the forty or so or hundred or so other dudes who've seen them. He liked them, but he didn't die over them. I guess it's the way you might figure out your dog doesn't like a certain brand of dog food. He's eating it, but you can tell he'd rather be going to town on something else. So after a few months it occurred to me that Mike must be a butt guy.[1] And that's when I became officially obsessed with looking at other women's butts. I leer at women's butts so openly on the street that I have essentially become a terribly rude man.

This newfound concern for my butt is how I found myself at a Bar Method studio about a year ago, on the recommendation of a friend who developed an eating disorder before her wedding. It is a class for women, or rather for women's problem areas. Women have problem areas in a way that men don't. We have big hips and muffin tops. Men just have the thing where they create wars and wreak havoc all over the globe.

Walking into Bar Method is not like walking into a normal gym. The lighting is warm and gentle. You immediately lose about three pounds just with the lighting. Cute girls work the front desk surrounded by bottles of SmartWater, which you can charge right on your account!!! Then there are the other women attending the classes. Everyone is in Lululemon. Everyone.

You check in and then you go into the spotless studio room and sit on the edge of the spongy white carpet and watch other girls casually do splits as they stretch. Everyone knows to grab two sets of tiny little weights the size and color of Tic Tacs. Finally, an instructor with a brond

---

1   He has never confirmed or denied any of this.

ponytail and a headset walks in and clicks on a sound system. Everyone faces the mirror and starts marching in place. It's time to begin.

Bar Method is an hour-long class of teeny-tiny movements where you hold on to a ballet barre and just...move...your...leg...an...inch...up and down...a thousand...times...and if you stick with it, over the course of many hours, you will have the perfect ass. A dancer's ass. It sounds ridiculous, but then you look at the butts of the teachers, who are also all in Lululemon, and you start to think maybe this is possible. None of them have a trapezoidal rear. Their butts are like the very best of the produce section. Juicy little fruits that stick out, suspended in midair, slappable, grabbable. Or so I imagine. I imagine what it would be like to be armed with a butt like this and be with a man, to feel the animal-like desire my new perfect butt would generate.

What does the perfect butt look like? Why would I even bother telling you when we all obviously know? Well, I suppose there are a few variations. There's the Lopez, a perfect big bubble. I've seen her in person; it's truly spectacular. Did you know that Julia Stiles also has this butt? I do, because I saw her at a Hampton Chutney Co.[2] with her boyfriend one Saturday morning and he could not stop touching it.

Then there's the waifier, smaller, perfect butt, which

---

2 If you don't know what Hampton Chutney Co. is that is fine. It is a small restaurant in New York City where they serve chutney.

is basically the shape of two tennis balls glued together. This butt is very common in Waspier enclaves and is often attached to a girl named Kim who wears an enormous amount of Tory Burch.

But I digress.

The biggest problem with Bar Method, other than everything about it, is that it's impossibly difficult. My friend Julie told me that a friend of hers once had to walk out in the middle to throw up. I'm impressed that she made it to the middle.

While I, too, feel the need to puke and cannot make it through a single set of inch-high mini squats without stopping, every other woman in this class is breezing through this torture like it's nothing, from the ones in their fifties who are barely breaking a sweat to the majority in their twenties who already have the tennis-ball butt. They are just here for maintenance. This leads me to a devastating realization: Despite having been surrounded by New York's population of beautiful women for most of my life, it had never occurred to me how incredibly FUCKING hard these women are working to look the way they do. No one ever told me. It's not just about going to the gym and doing the elliptical for forty minutes.[3] It's about taking a class where you are in horrible pain and hate your life and might lose your lunch at any moment.

---

3 I'd naively always thought that being on the elliptical meant I was exercising. It does not. Women who are in great shape, the women who really work out, consider being on the elliptical something akin to a nap.

And as I study these women holding their squats for minutes at a time, it dawns on me that they must have started doing this when they were teenagers. These women, with their flat stomachs and the lines down their quads and the skinny jeans that fit perfectly, have been chiseling, toning, chipping, and whittling since forever. I hadn't known that this is what it takes to have an acceptable body. I feel like I'll never catch up.

There are so many miserable things about Bar Method, it's hard to know where to begin. Well:

First of all, the instructor wears a headset microphone. I'm not exactly sure why this bothers me so much, but on some level it makes me feel like we're all taking this way too seriously. This is not a Madonna concert. The room is not that large. We would definitely hear her without the microphone but she is determined to wear it. It also evokes one of my huge pet peeves, which is when a famous actor directs a short film for the first time and it's very important they have their picture taken with a headset around their neck so we know they are DIRECTING.

Furthermore, all the instructors have an uncanny ability to memorize the name of every woman in the class and will use it to humiliating effect when they correct you over the microphone: "Jessi, tuck your seat." Everyone looks over to see who this shitty seat tucker is. The first time I ever took the class there was another Jessi there, clearly someone who had earned enough Bar Method hours that she now had the dignity of going by first name only, and so I was the one stuck with "Jessi

Klein." Over and over again, the teacher would curtly say into her fucking headset, "Jessi Klein, lower your shoulders. Jessi Klein, deepen the tuck in your seat." Just in case anyone wants to be able to track down the muffintoppy girl with terrible form, her full name is Jessi Klein.

Did I mention that in this class your butt is always referred to as "your seat"? Can you imagine anything creepier than this? It's oddly neutered, somewhere in between medical and infantilizing. It's only slightly better than "tushy."

Then there's the Bar Method music. Like the class itself, it is joyless. Of the one dillion hip-hop, rap, soul, punk, and R&B songs in the world that would be fun to move to, they have opted for none of them. Instead they have selected (and I think created?) a kind of ambient, stripped-down beat, the sort of sound that used to come out of my brother's Casio synthesizer circa 1985. (There were a few buttons you could push that would lay down the foundational bass for "samba," "tango," "rock," and I think also "polka.")

On top of all this, there is the price. It costs $36 a class. Thirty-six bucks! That means it's $72 for two classes. Bar Method suggests that for optimal results you do the class five times a week.

That's $180 a week you'd be spending on your ASS.

The saddest fact about Bar Method, however—the most heartbreaking, annoying, decimating thing about it—is this: It works. After taking maybe about seven classes, I went to my waxer, Rivka. Rivka has been up in my most personal physical business for a decade now, and when I say she has seen parts of my body that I never have in my entire life, I am not exaggerating. Every three weeks I go to her for what is essentially 80 percent of the way to a colonoscopy. The point is, she knows me. I was lying on the table on my stomach (don't ask, it's all so unspeakably gross) when suddenly Rivka gasped. "Why does your butt look so good?" Rivka is a boundary-less Russian Jew who has more than once demanded to see my tits because she's considering getting a boob job and wants to get some ideas. She's in her late thirties and very pretty, although she occasionally seems shrouded in a kind of mysterious ennui, although I suppose it's really not all that mysterious because, let's face it, waxing other people's pussies can't exactly add years to your life.

Anyway, I tell her it's not possible. My butt looks the same, I'm sure. But she is adamant. "Everything looks tighter," she insists, and then she gives it a little slap.

Later that night at home, I start telling Mike what Rivka said. He's in bed reading and seems not to be paying attention to what I'm saying about my trip to the waxer (fair enough), but he perks up when I mention her comment, and for the first time puts down his reading.

"It's true," he says.

"What do you mean," I press.

"It looks tighter. It feels tighter." He goes back to his reading.

Well, fuck me.

This is both the best news and the worst news.

Do I have to keep going now? I don't want to. I don't want to worry about my ass while I march in place. I want to go forward, and forget all about it.

Poodle vs. Wolf

One late night when I was working at *SNL*, I wandered out of my office for a break and saw that some random TV in the hallway was tuned to an interview with Angelina Jolie (I think it was with Charlie Rose, who was shamelessly hitting on her, as is his wont when he interviews a pretty lady). I wandered over to watch, as did Emily, one of the senior writers there at the time and an all-around hilarious and fabulous lady. We both stared at Angelina in awe.

"Isn't it amazing," Emily asked, "that we're the same species she is? It doesn't even feel like we are the same species."

"I know," I said. I continued the riff: It's like with dogs. A poodle and a wolf are both technically dogs, but based on appearances, it doesn't make any conceivable sense that they share a common ancestor. We decided that some women are poodles and some women are wolves. And no matter what a wolf does (puts on makeup, or a thong), it will still be a wolf, and no matter what a poodle does (puts on sweatpants), it will always be a poodle.

CLASSIC POODLE-WOLF MOMENT #1

I am on my way to meet my friend Tracy for breakfast and decide to wear my new dress, which I love, a black dress with white butterflies and pockets[1] from Agnès B., which is a pricey French retail chain that represented the highest echelons of fanciness to me as a kid. I had never gone in, ever. But a couple of months earlier I was drawn in by the butterfly dress, and looking in the mirror I thought I looked really pretty and girlie, like Zooey Deschanel but from EUROPE, and decided to spend an ungodly amount of cash on this poodle feeling I had.

So I enter the subway in my butterfly dress and start to walk slowly to one end of the platform, waiting for men's heads to turn while I practice saying in my head, "Take a picture, it'll last longer," even though no one is looking. And then this other woman walks in right behind me, and everything changes.

She is clearly a dancer, or a former dancer, but who cares, look at her, she has long perfect legs that are all one tawny color, not a speckled mixture of wintergreens and veiny blues like mine are, and she is wearing short jean shorts and a plain denim shirt, and her hair is sloppily piled on top of her head with a cheap clip. She is

---

1   Seeing pockets on a dress is now the sartorial equivalent of finding out that a guy has a giant dick. When women show up at the Oscars with their hands in their pockets and get interviewed, Giuliana Rancic is like "Oh my Gawwwd, look, POCKETS!" and then Amy Adams is like "I know, I love pockets!"

stunning. You can feel everyone's energy shift as all men on the platform cycle through their quick glance-up/ glance-away thing that they think will keep them from being caught looking.[2]

I then do the secret embarrassing thing of purposely getting on the same subway car as her so I can keep looking at a pretty person. I'm not a lesbian, but looking at her gives me a feeling of pleasure. I study her face. She is wearing red lipstick and looks basically like Mena Suvari at the exact moment in *American Beauty* that Kevin Spacey fantasizes about fucking her on a bed of rose petals.

This woman is a classic poodle. By which I mean, she is effortless. It doesn't matter what she is wearing, as this woman isn't especially stylish. But because she's a poodle she looks good in anything. She will always look like an ocean breeze, short of donning a Nazi uniform on Halloween (and even then, you'd forgive her just that one time because it's Halloween and she's so pretty and that means she's a good person who didn't mean it). When someone is a poodle, you just want to be near her. My own attempt at poodleness suddenly seems like a silly farce, as it is obvious I am just a wolf in poodle's clothing. My butterfly Agnès B. dress with pockets may as well be a ziplock bag filled with old shrimp.

Does this all sound too self-deprecating? Because I don't mean it to be. It's just that I am in awe of poodles,

---

2   We catch you looking. We always catch you looking.

these magical lovely women who inherently radiate femininity. They are not necessarily the most beautiful women or even the prettiest; they just seem, without trying at all, to always be in sync with their yin quality (that's the girl one, right?), like an iPhone in constant communication with its cloud.

If you're still confused about what a poodle is, just think about this: "The Girl from Ipanema" was obviously written about a poodle. No one would ever write that song about a wolf.

Famous Poodle Women:

Angelina Jolie
Keira Knightley
Charlize Theron
Kate Moss
Nigella Lawson

Famous Wolf Women:

Sandra Bullock
Helena Bonham Carter
Tina Fey
Jennifer Aniston

Jennifer Aniston is actually an interesting example here. I have friends who think she is a poodle and argue that the reason she is a poodle is that she's beautiful. And she is beautiful. BUT BEING BEAUTIFUL IS NOT WHAT MAKES YOU A POODLE OR A WOLF. There are millions of beautiful wolf women out there. It's how much of the beauty feels like work, like maintenance. It's a very French concept, which is probably why we think every actual poodle was born in France and we always imagine them in berets. Aniston is stunning, but I always have the impression that her beauty comes with an enormous price tag. Getting your hair to be the color of a sunbeam passing through a lion's mane don't come cheap. And yes, in Hollywood everyone's beauty is expensive, but there are a few ladies who seem like they're keeping very high tabs permanently open at every groomer in town. And yes, Janiston would be stunningly beautiful even if she did nothing, but it's the fact that she chooses to do EVERYTHING that tells me she's a wolf. If you look at her high school yearbook picture, where she has thick eyebrows and an (ever so slightly) bigger nose, you can see she felt like a wolf. I'm certain she still feels like one. She'd probably feel like a wolf no matter what happened in her life—once a wolf always a wolf—but nothing will really make you feel like a wolf like your husband leaving you for a poodle.

Natasha Lyonne is a wolf. I'm pretty sure Kristen Bell is a wolf.

Sofía Vergara is a poodle, duh.

I have always clearly been a wolf. I grew up knowing nothing about manicures or pedicures or embellished bras. When I got my period at age thirteen, my mother gave me that crazy elastic belt thingy that women used in the 1950s with a weird pad that had extra fabric at both ends so you could tie it onto the plastic clips that dangled from the belt. Most of the readers who would know what I'm talking about here are probably dead. Somehow, my mom—who despite having two daughters failed to pay attention to advances in menstrual technology—completely missed the fact that there were other options. So I wore the belt for about a year, until I finally noticed the football-field-length aisle of modern maxi pads at CVS. Then I used exclusively pads until I was twenty-seven because my mother never said anything about tampons. And this only changed because of a trip to the beach with my then-boyfriend, where I had to choose between not going into the ocean and exploring this newfangled tampon technology. I FINALLY bought a box of tampons and looked at the diagram and pushed one in, no problem, no fuss no muss, and felt a flash of anger at my mother that I had wasted more than a decade walking around wearing a mini diaper every time I menstruated.

But when I think back on it, really, it was unavoidable. We were a wolf family.

Poodle Characteristics:

Poodles are confident.
Poodles are always late.
Poodles laugh a lot!!!

Poodles always wear matching bras and underwear.
Poodles lose their virginity in high school.

CLASSIC POODLE-WOLF MOMENT #2

I live near a very nice park that runs along the water.
There is a cluster of picnic tables where I will occasionally go to write if the weather is nice. The other morning
it was brilliantly sunny out and I grabbed my laptop and
headed over. I was hunched in front of my screen and enjoying an iced coffee when I noticed a kerfuffle at one
of the picnic tables about forty feet away. Seven or so
people were setting up a fashion shoot around a female
model, but they didn't seem to be asking anyone to move,
so I went back to my writing. About ten minutes later,
the photographer, a handsome Frenchman (male poodle?), came over and gently asked if I could move over
about two feet because I was in the background of the
shot. I looked around and saw that there were a few other
bystanders who looked as if they might also be in the
background of the shot. But I was the only one who had to
move. I understood. I moved and watched them take pictures of the poodle.

YOU CAN'T HAVE A WOLF IN THE SHOT.

Wolf Characteristics:

Wolves need to eat more than poodles do (both
larger amounts and more frequently).

Wolves wear lip balm.

Wolves can't deal with thongs.

Wolves sweat a lot.

Wolves are funny.

Wolves show up ten minutes early to everything and are always the first ones there and then have to fake a conversation on their cell phones so they look like they know other human beings on this earth.

Wolves usually own two bras total, and neither of them matches their tattered old Gap underwear.

Wolves lose their virginity during their junior year of college at the very earliest.

I often wonder, if I could wave a wand and magically transform myself from a wolf to a poodle, would I? Most of me says no. I'm proud of being a wolf. My wolf upbringing is responsible for my personality, for my compassion for the rest of the pack. As a wolf, I'm a diamond in the rough. I crack jokes. My whole life is about trying, about speaking up in order to be seen, about howling with laughter or howling out how I see the world.

But there is another part of me that immediately yells, Yes, I would give anything to feel that poodle confidence, to feel comfortable as a woman, like my body is my perfect home, to be the girl from Ipanema and sway down the street emitting an intoxicating hormone, like a female deer spritzing the air from under my perky white tail. I'd love to be one of those women who sleeps naked, who never has to buy her own drink, who wears makeup only when she feels like it, who took ballet for years and still carries that motion in her bones, dancing down the street, never a bad angle, completely unself-conscious.

The Cad

While men spend most of their romantic energy pursuing the hottest possible women who will have them, we ladies invest more of our energy thinking about whether any particular man measures up to a more widely encompassing set of "standards." These include, but are not limited to, how he will treat us in general, whether he brushes his teeth at night in addition to in the morning, whether he asks our friends questions, whether he knows to keep the perimeter of his bed free of balled-up jerk-off tissues when we come over.

But when you are young and innocent, if you've had a decent enough childhood with some semblance of loving parents (or parent), you don't really think too much about standards. This is because you assume everyone will meet them. Standards are something you accumulate over a lifetime of interacting with potential romantic partners and figuring out, as you encounter new bullshit, what is bullshit you will tolerate and what is undeniably deal-breaker bullshit. We generally see holes in our friends' standards before we see holes in ours. When we were in high school, my friend Maggie met a guy named Saffron (name has not been changed) who was very cute but struck me as being a little…simple.

One day after school we were sitting at our local diner and Saffron noticed my pro-choice button, the one with a red line over a hanger.

"What do you have against hangers?" Saffron asked.

He was serious.

Maggie needed higher standards.

By the time I was thirty-three I thought I'd curated a very solid set of standards. Since my life-changing breakup I'd dated, in addition to a group of very good dudes, an assortment of dullards, weirdos, and withholders. Every time I would part ways with one of those guys, I would fine-tune my standards to exclude their category from my future explorations.

And yet, at some point in every woman's life, she dates a cad. Someone who consistently fails to meet every rule you've carefully cultivated over the years as to how you will permit yourself to be treated. My friend Tami describes this condition as "being lost on the Shutter Island of good dick" because you are under the sway of a powerful and confusing force.

I thought I might possibly escape this fate because I was nerdy and academic and went to Vassar and in general considered myself immune to cads, whom I pictured looking like James Spader in *Pretty in Pink*, all blazers and loafers with no socks and *GQ*ish looks. I liked chubby shlubs with hairy arms and beat-up Converse. I didn't like vain guys, or guys with too much style, or guys with money.

Then I met Damon.

My friend Henry is the one who set us up. I wish I could blame the whole thing on him, but that wouldn't be fair. He is responsible for about one-thirtieth of it, insofar as anyone else who knew this person, including friends of his who were even closer to him than Henry, knew what a bad idea it was to date him. Maybe Henry's responsible for two-thirtieths.

But I wasn't really looking for something serious. (I swear, I really wasn't.) This is how unserious I was: I was living in LA, where I was finding even casual dating to be impossible. I was lonely and, I apologize in advance for using this word…horny. (Is there any word worse than *horny*? No, there isn't.) One night (probably drunk) I started texting with an ex of mine, Luke, someone I hadn't seen in at least five years. Silly sexy ex texting in which we slowly established that:

1. We were both single;
2. We were both horny and lonely; and
3. We were both apparently willing to go backward in our lives in order to get a temporary fix of human contact.

I had a week off from work approaching, and I'm ashamed to admit that I hatched a "plan" to fly to New York, where

Luke lived, spend the week having sex with him, and then return to LA. I acknowledge that this was less of a "plan" and more of a "bad idea." And I am not proud of the fact that I was going to travel thousands of miles to have intercourse. I'm even less proud of the fact that at that point in my life, it wasn't even the most miles I'd ever flown to have sex with a person.[1]

I got to New York and quickly wrangled a rendezvous with Luke. He was in a different, bigger apartment since the last time we'd dated, but despite the change in space and some updated furniture, the vibe—midcentury emotionally withholding—remained the same. By the second day of hanging out, we were already having the exact same kind of fight that had broken us up in the first place. We had lunch at a panini bar, started bickering as we ate mozzarella with red peppers, and parted ways in a mutual huff. We didn't see each other again until I ran into him on the street years later, just weeks before his wedding.

In the midst of this failed reunion, my friend Henry had mentioned Damon. "I have someone you could have lunch with," he wrote. "Worst-case scenario, you'd be friends." This is what people always say when they are setting you up. That the worst thing that could come from meeting up would be a friendship. It is a lie. There are so many much much worse things that could happen. Off the top of my head, I'm thinking murder, rape, a broken heart, theft, to name but a few.

---

1   That would be about 3,500 miles.

But I was intrigued by his description. Damon was a green architect, which sounded sophisticated. It's the kind of job desirable men have in movies, and yet you never meet them in real life. He lived three blocks from my New York apartment and had been divorced about a year. I had never dated a divorced guy, which was like being a bird-watcher and never having seen a fairly common variety of bird, a bird your other bird-watching friends would occasionally mention they'd been fucked over by.

Okay, I told Henry. Lunch.

Damon emailed me. It was one of those flirty first emails that landed perfectly in the place between being humorous and trying too hard that only a few people really nail, but he did it. He suggested a few places to meet, all of them perfect foodie choices—the Spotted Pig, Joseph Leonard, Waverly Inn. Places with brick walls and antique chairs. We decided on the Spotted Pig. He walked in and, in an all-too-infrequent miracle, looked like his picture. My one fear had been that he would be super short (I don't mean to make short men feel bad, I am just fairly tall for a female and thus have that embarrassing emotional need to be with a taller man so I can experience the feminine feeling of being the tiniest most delicate princess in the world, basically Thumbelina), but he was a normal height.

We ordered red meat and cheese and drank tons of red wine until we were both laughing at jokes that were only a little funny. He had a deep voice but spoke softly, in a way that made you lean in to hear him. We talked about architecture and design and even a little about his divorce. Overall, he was delightful. The only thing that threw me off slightly was that I noticed he was wearing loafers with no socks. Deep in my gut, some ancient female cosmic wisdom was whispering to me that this was not okay. But I ignored it.

I do not intend this in any way to be an advice book, but if there happen to be any young women reading this who have an iota of desire to glean anything from my experience, let it be this: When you encounter a man wearing loafers with no socks, run. I once heard that the late Tim Russert also believed that a sockless man is not to be trusted, which means it is definitively true.

We parted ways with a polite hug around four in the afternoon, and I went back to the weird extra room in my parents' house where I was staying and lay down on the bed to enjoy my wine buzz. An hour and a half later, I checked my email. There was a message from Damon. "Wanna get an after-dinner drink?" I was ecstatic in the way you get when you are certain someone has just fallen very hard in love with you and is currently scribbling their first name with your last name in the margins of a notebook. Two drinks in one day! Magic! I went to meet him at another bar.

More red wine and more drunkenness followed until we kissed next to one of those NYC garbage-bag mountains and then he asked if I wanted to go home with him.

Deciding I didn't want to come off as too easy, I declined. After all, I have standards.

So we had sex the next day.

It was a different kind of sex than I'd had in the past. I had always laughed at that stupid cheesy John Mayer song "Your Body Is a Wonderland," but as we tumbled naked on his bed, I started to think for the first time that perhaps this guy was thinking MY body was a wonderland. I had never thought of myself as having a "wonderland" body, but that was the vibe he was giving off. More than anything, I was excited that my sex trip plan had taken this unexpected detour. I'd never had a one-night stand before, and this felt close enough. I was going back to LA on Monday, on an eight a.m. flight, and assumed I would never see him again. I felt like such a grown-up. I did my own taxes, I had health insurance, and I was having casual sex. So incredibly casual. I barely knew this guy! I was an adult!

And that was the end of my first and only attempt at a one-night stand. And also, as I would soon learn, my standards.

We started writing each other all the time. He was always funny and charming and would tell me self-deprecating tales of his most recent failed attempts at jogging. I would write back with exaggerated tales of how silly Los Angeles was and how much I was day-drinking. He would respond with emails saying he kinda wished I was in New York (and then there would be an asterisk, and at the bottom of the email, the asterisk would indicate that after typing that sentence he'd gone to hide under the bed, ablush. That kind of endearing bullshit). We were falling into the exciting tingle of fake intimacy through email, where a few personal overshares, blended with a sprinkling of coy, overly specific compliments, mimic the sensation of falling in love (when in fact usually you are only falling in love with yourself and your ability to write a really top-notch flirty email).

One morning I woke up, and my inbox was empty. No email from him. I panicked. I consulted my work friend Jim about how to time my responses back. He wanted to know more about Damon before answering. I showed him all of Damon's emails.

"What do you think?" I asked.

Jim, a married father of two and an ultimate mensch, was underwhelmed. "He seems pretty into himself," he said.

"Whatever, but is it better to write again or wait for him to write back?" I asked.

Jim, like any sane person, advised not writing until Damon did, and even then skipping a day or two before responding. I did as Jim said, and of course, it worked. I didn't write him for two days and then, magically, in his very next email he told me he was coming out to Los Angeles in a few weeks, glomming on to a work trip with a good friend to share a hotel room, and would I want to hang out?

!!!

It seemed OBVIOUS and VERY CLEAR he was using

his friend's trip as an excuse to come see me. I began elaborate preparations for our tryst.

I waxed. I made an itinerary of my favorite things to do in LA (there weren't many). I bought some new outfits. I cleaned my house. I bought a shit ton of booze. I went to Trader Joe's and bought one of those large bags filled with many smaller bags of almonds. I bought crackers and the fanciest cheeses I could find (at Trader Joe's). At work, a few days before his arrival, I began to plant the seeds of the idea that I wasn't feeling well, so that I could believably call in sick and spend the day with ~~my new boyfriend~~ him the morning after he landed. Jim looked at me with weary side eye as I mused aloud in front of the writers room about my "sore throat."

Damon texted me from the plane when they touched down. We met up that night at Chateau Marmont, where he was staying with his friend, and had another boozy dinner. Afterward, we drove back to my apartment. I showed him around my sublet, making my usual jokes about the lesbian-centric furnishings (I was renting from a lesbian) and the high number of AIDS-related books (she was a doctor specializing in AIDS treatment). Midway through the tour, we tumbled into bed. Everything was going well when he whispered into my ear, would it be okay if we didn't use a condom?

This is where my standards should have kicked in. This is also where it gets embarrassing.

I grew up in the '80s and thus was trained from an early age to avoid dying of two things: a crack overdose and AIDS. I watched more teachers slip more condoms onto more bananas than I could count. As a result, I was a condom Nazi. At no point in my life had I ever allowed a ~~murder weapon~~ penis to come near me unless it was sheathed, and ideally also medically tested and approved. And yet for some reason, at this moment, I was weak. Agh, it is so embarrassing to tell you what I was thinking but I will tell you what I was thinking. In my head, the only reason he would ask me such a thing, when we'd known each other for such a short time— oh fuck, this is genuinely so humiliating, but I want this book to be nothing but the FACTS—the only reason I could generate, in the middle of movie sex with this guy who had so very obviously flown across the country just to see me—was that he already knew he was falling in love with me and knew he wanted to be in a committed relationship with me.[2]

I know I know I know I know.

But in that moment, surrounded by AIDS books, I said okay. What did it matter if we didn't use a condom if we were never going to be with other people again?

The next morning, I woke up, aglow[3] and ready to hatch my hooky plan. It was an ideal LA day, the California morning light shining gently through my windows.

I said, "I'm gonna call in sick to work."

He said, "You are?"

---

2 Runs and hides under bed, ablush.*
3 In heavy denial.

I replied, "Yeah, it's no big deal."

He then watched me as I called the writers' assistant to pass along the message that I was "severely" "under" "the weather" and would be an infectious danger to all around me. I hung up the phone, a naughty, triumphant gleam in my eye.

Then, as I settled back into bed, he looked at me and said, "I actually have a bunch of stuff I have to do today."

Whaaaaaaa?

"I promised Rob that I would go to his shoot with him. Then I'm supposed to meet Nevill for tennis in the afternoon. But we could have dinner?"

I was dumbstruck. He had watched me pick up the phone and make the call.

I decided I had to pretend it was okay, and attempted an impossible emotional pivot wherein I acted like taking the day off was something I'd been planning on doing even if he hadn't been there.

Even now, sitting here thinking about that moment and trying to write about it, the awkwardness of this inter-action is staggering. The way we both behaved was staggering. His incredible insensitivity, my dedication to the completely nonsensical idea that I was just sick of work and was planning on taking a day for some "me time." I suppose that was the moment when we both realized the misunderstanding that had occurred. He suddenly real-ized, *This girl thinks I am here to see her*, and I suddenly realized, *I'm really fucking stupid*. He kissed me good-bye and left, promising we'd meet for dinner and walking out just a touch more quickly than was necessary for what sounded like a leisurely schedule.

The rest of the day unspooled in slow motion, every unexpected free minute snailing along like it was an hour. Los Angeles is a lonely city, and the oppressive isolation of it can usually only be avoided through careful social planning. I went for coffee at the sad Starbucks around the corner and then straightened up my house. After those two activities, I was out of ideas. I started calling my freelancer and unemployed friends, seeing if I could arrange a lunch date. My friend Jenny could only meet if I drove to her in Santa Monica, a place that is deathly to drive to from Hollywood at lunchtime, but in this case I agreed since my "romantic lunchtime hike," along with all my other plans, had been scrubbed from my calendar.

At lunch, I told Jenny about what had happened. Jenny is an eternally optimistic and sunny person, but in this case, I could see her struggling to find a positive reaction.

"Hmm," she said. "Has he been in touch since this morning?"

He hadn't.

He would continue to not be in touch as I drove through an hour of pudding-like traffic on the way back from lunch, as I watched *Oprah*, as I drank half a bottle of wine in the kitchen. The clock ticked its way to five, and I started to soften as I thought, *Well, it's almost dinnertime. We had a genuine miscommunication. We'll go get something to eat soon. We still have the whole weekend.*

Then it was six and seven and he still didn't call.

I had never been stood up before. My feelings were hurt. What hurt the most was the knowledge that the guy who was standing me up had also, most likely, given me full-blown AIDS just the night before.

Finally, around seven thirty, he texted—not called—to let me know he was driving to see his friend Rowan, a nice guy I randomly happened to be acquainted with as well. He'd promised Rowan he would stop by, and now he was in bad traffic, and anyway he would be in touch very soon.

Forty minutes later, my cell phone rang. The caller ID was unfamiliar. I picked up the phone. It wasn't Damon, but instead Rowan.

"Hey, Damon wanted me to call you," he said.

"Is he dead?" I fantasized about asking.

"What's going on?" I asked in real life.

"He wanted me to ask if you wanted to come over for dinner," he replied. He went on to try, unsuccessfully, to explain why he was on the phone and Damon was not. Here is where I should also mention that Damon was not twenty-two years old. He was almost forty. He had put me in the humiliating position of having to communicate with him through a mutual friend, a friend who could clearly tell I had been cuckolded. (I know this is not technically the definition of the word *cuckolded* but it's a fun word and it somehow feels right in this context.)

This was yet another opportunity where my standards could have kicked in.

* * *

In retrospect, the misunderstanding about the plan was forgivable—I was responsible for constructing a fantasy of what the day was—but the genuine asshattery on his part was not picking up the phone to call me. Really, the only right thing for me to do at that moment would have been to delete his number from my phone, make a bowl of spaghetti, and watch *Weeds*.

But then he started texting me. Texting is like kryptonite to women's standards. It erodes them, like gentle ocean waves slowly, over time, destroy a beautiful dune. Could we meet up later? he asked. He was going to meet Henry for a drink after dinner, did I want to join them? He really wanted to see me. Please come. Please please. Really really really…

Shutter Island of Dick. The confusion set in.

I decided I would have it both ways. I would go to meet them, but I would still be really angry, and I would be nice to everyone but Damon, and *then* wouldn't he be sorry? There is nothing that makes men want to fall in line more than a mopey passive-aggressive chick, am I right ladiezzz? I am aware this was not the decision of a grown-ass woman, but rather the immature, fevered thinking of a small-ass, hurt child.

There were a few other friends gathered when I arrived at Henry's beautiful Laurel Canyon home. Everyone was listening to Harry Nilsson on vinyl and drinking scotch. I took a seat as far from Damon as possible and did some of my finest acting work as I pretended to be fascinated by the guy sitting next to me. I could sense Damon occasionally looking at me, and I felt the smug satisfaction of the deeply righteous and imagined his excruciating guilt. *Surely*, I thought, *he is feeling that special kind of remorse that jolts you into realizing you are in love with someone.* I did not know at the time that there are no recorded instances of a man ever feeling this, ever in all of history.

Afterward, a bunch of us piled into Damon's friend's car to get rides home. His hotel was just a few blocks from where I lived. He leaned over and whisper-asked if he was coming back to my house. A snap decision had to be made about whether he was staying over.

The "me" I knew before I met Damon would have quickly perused her standards pamphlet and known that the answer should be no. But this was a new, shittier me, whose standards were slowly fading from view.

What I was thinking was that I would have it both ways again. Keep this amazing uncomfortable vibe going. Have him come back home with me, but confront him about what happened. Not let him off the hook. By which I also mean, I didn't want to let him go. I didn't want to be alone. I really, genuinely liked him.

We got out of the car in front of my house and stood on the sidewalk. He looked at me, a confused almost-smile on his face. "Is everything okay?" he asked.

"Why do you think it's not?" I replied. I was a genius.

"Your feelings for me seem to have cooled since this morning," he said.

At that point I asked him why he even cared how I felt. To which he replied, "I just want you to like me."

The biggest difference between me now and me then is that back then, I didn't clock what was wrong with that sentence. I heard "I" and "like" and I invited him in, even though I was still mad, and even though I didn't want him to think I was okay enough with what happened to have sex with him again, which I did.

It wasn't until months later, when I was even more deeply entangled with him, and had been hurt umpteen more times, that I looked at that moment differently. I realized that "I just want you to like me" was not in any way related to "I like you." He was the object, the person looking to be liked. Whether or not he liked me was beside the point.

This was a revelation. I had heard girls talk about the perils of dating a "narcissist," but I had never truly known what that meant and was not familiar with the personality profile. It wasn't until I sheepishly started taking online quizzes titled "Are You Dating a Narcissist?" and getting A+ results on all of them that I realized I was most definitely dating a narcissist.

As soon as I opened my eyes the next morning, I felt a wave of regret. When he woke up, I made up a lie about having to get to a Pilates class (if he'd known me any better, it would have been obvious just what a huge lie that was) and ushered him out the door. I called my friend Tracy, a talented writer and my longtime unofficial relationship guru.

"He needs to man up and let you know he understands what he did wrong," she declared at breakfast. I nodded vigorously into a glass of white wine the size of an adult cat.

"How will I know that he really understands?" I asked.

"He'll make a gesture," she said.

A gesture. I'd never really dated men who'd made gestures. I'd gotten some flowers here and there on the usual mandatory occasions—Valentine's Day, wisdom teeth being extracted—but I had never been with a guy who had made a genuinely thoughtful, romantic gesture.

Tracy went on to remind me that a man having his friend call you after bailing on plans was substandard behavior. "Men rise to the standards you hold them up to," she explained. "Their behavior will always be at the exact bar you allow it to be."

I bought Tracy breakfast. I felt like I owed her a lot more than a poached egg and a salad for words of advice I would carry with me for the rest of my life. But sometimes you get a bargain.

I spent the rest of the day icing Damon, who again responded with a series of increasingly panicky texts. Not responding to the texts of a man who has wronged you is truly one of the sweetest pleasures in life. In the evening I met up with my guy friend Eric and we drove to a delicious but slightly sad Mexican restaurant in Echo Park, where I told him everything that had happened. Eric agreed that what had occurred was not amazing, but ventured that maybe there was still hope. He had the heterosexual optimism of a man who has never dated another man.

On my drive home, Damon's texts continued to trickle in. He wanted to know if we could get lunch the next day. I thought about saying no. But I decided I wouldn't "play games." We'd get lunch, and I'd be open about how hurt I was, and I would explain that I wanted him to make a gesture. To be clear, Tracy had not recommended that last part. But I was worried that if I didn't ask for this thing I wanted, I wouldn't get it. And how else would he understand what I needed? How else would he come up with this idea? The notion that perhaps he should realize it on his own seemed too dicey even to consider.

We went to lunch at the same place Tracy and I had dined, the restaurant at Fred Segal, a ridiculously LA place where skinny LA people eat overpriced salads before going to buy overpriced skinny jeans at the adjacent boutique. I ordered spaghetti. I think I am the only person who ever ordered pasta there. I would not be surprised if a memorial plaque was placed on my chair, thanking me for my service.

Damon ordered a bottle of rosé that was put in a bucket of ice next to our table. Anytime you have a bottle of booze in ice next to your table it feels like everything must be simpatico because look at this fun bucket of ice! Life's a party!

Or at least, life was a party until I started explaining to him why what he'd done had made me feel bad. The explaining did not go particularly well. His resting face was generally "bemused/quizzical," and as I spoke it only grew more so. We drove back to my house, where we sat on my patio, drinking more rosé, and continued the conversation. He wasn't defensive exactly—it was more like he couldn't wrap his head around the concept of himself as an agent of unpleasant feelings in anyone else. He got held up throughout his day on Friday, he said, and then traffic was bad. He'd promised Rowan he would stop by, and so he had to do that. Whatever negative effect his actions may have had on me, it was as if he couldn't find the language necessary to discuss it.

When I brought up the idea of a gesture, his look went from bemused to full shar-pei, his brow was so furrowed in confusion. It is remarkable to me now that I was so willing to try to dictate to this person the behavior I wanted him to mimic; when I think back on it, I cringe. And this wasn't the only time it happened. When I moved back to New York, I remember sitting with him on my couch, after he'd chipped my heart in some other small way, and literally showing him a dog-eared page from Greg Behrendt's classic tome, *He's Just Not That Into You.* It posited that if a man you're dating isn't treating you like he loves you, it means he does not really love you, and you should leave. (It definitely did not suggest that you show him pages from your worn copy of a self-help book as a way of convincing him to stay.)

But I digress.

We are on the porch. I tell him about gestures. About how they indicate a depth of feeling when it comes to such notions as affection and apologies. And how it might be nice if he made one. He sipped more rosé and put his hand on my knee. I remember thinking that seemed like a good start. I forgave him, overlooking the fact that he hadn't apologized. We ordered crappy takeout for dinner and laughed about our stomachaches when we tried to go to sleep. I shared the last of my chewable Mylanta mints with him, crunching on them till both our tongues turned aquamarine.

He was going back to New York the next afternoon, and I gave him the key so he could let himself out, showing him the secret hiding place under the doormat[4] where he could stash it when he left. We kissed good-bye. Even though the weekend had not unspooled in the exact manner I'd planned, I wanted to believe it had led us to a deeper understanding. I felt good that I had stood my ground and made it clear I was not to be trifled with. In hindsight, I had in fact done none of those things, and I understood literally zero about anything.

But that night, as I returned home from work, I was driven by the excitement of finding the gesture that would surely be waiting for me somewhere on the premises. I went from room to room, first scanning the obvious places—the kitchen table, the sofa, my desk. Then—and again it is horrible that I must confess this, I

---

4   I am aware this is a terrible hiding place. This is where you should hide your key if you want to make sure all your possessions are taken from your home while you are at your job.

am disgusting—I started looking under things. I looked under the blanket on my bed, in the medicine cabinet, in the refrigerator. I don't know why I was behaving so manically, or why I felt so certain that he would have done what I asked.

But the thing is, I wasn't wrong. After twenty minutes of frantic searching, I found it. It was actually on top of the refrigerator, not inside. But I finally saw the little brown paper bag resting atop his business card. I reached in and pulled out a new bottle of chewable Mylanta mints. I looked at his business card—good stock, classy font, letterpress. I flipped it over, and in all-caps he had written, "IT'S A GESTURE!"

What should I have learned from this? That his gesture was, in fact, telling me exactly who he was? That he would always be the source of a stomachache? That ironic gifts are a red flag? That when I periodically went through all the Facebook photos he was tagged in, it should have been clear to me that I wasn't the only girl he was sleeping with? That four months later, after several more cross-country rendezvous, after I invited him to accompany me to a comedy festival in Seattle where I was performing, I shouldn't have been surprised to discover, when I pulled off his underwear, that there were about fifteen mysterious little white bumps all around his penis? That I should have asked about the bumps right away, instead of waiting through two more days of sexual activity, because his silence about them made me feel embarrassed to say anything? Or maybe I should have learned that when I finally did ask him about the bumps, and asked if he'd been having unprotected sex with other girls, of course he would say yes, and that the worst part about it was that I knew I'd been lying to myself way more than he had. And then I could have gleaned that when we got back to New York, and he went to the doctor to get checked out, and I was lying in bed waiting for his phone call to confirm or deny that the bumps were herpes, that I shouldn't have expected him to call me as soon as he left. That if his appointment was at two p.m., and I hadn't heard from him by five, of course he had gone to get a drink with a friend, rather than calling me right away to tell me that we were in the clear, and in fact the bumps were a benign fungal infection acquired from a rented kilt he'd recently worn while on a business trip in Scotland.[5]

What I did learn was how easily my standards could go out the window when I met a man whose charm made me weak. Even after the bumpy penis and the hours of not calling to tell me the status of my health, I'm embarrassed to say our relationship still didn't end until a few weeks later, when I went to his apartment late at night and asked him if he thought we could try really dating just each other, just to see. We were lying in his bed, and I felt sure he'd say yes. Despite everything, we had so much fun together. We made each other laugh and had inside jokes and could talk about anything.

He said no, he didn't think he was ready.

---

5   I recognize that in many ways this is grosser than an actual STD.

But he still definitely wanted me to stay over.

I got up and told him that I actually had to go home.

There was one last bit of business to sort out between us. He'd asked me a few weeks earlier if I would accompany him on an all-expenses-paid trip to Tokyo, where he was meeting with a potential client. I agonized over the decision. Maybe I was being too hard on him. Of course he wasn't ready to be monogamous; he'd been through this horrible divorce. Maybe he just needed more time. If we went on this trip we would grow closer, and he would see that I could be trusted.

He had described himself to me, over and over, as a wounded bird, and I took him seriously. I truly thought it was my responsibility to nurse him back to health.

I thought this until I once again turned to my dear friend Jim, who'd been skeptical since the beginning, for advice, and he wrote me the following wise words in an email:

"Take care of your own bird."

I didn't go on the trip. I sent him a good-bye email, and we never spoke again.

I wrote "take care of your own bird" on a Post-it note that I stuck above my desk. I didn't take it down till four years later, when Mike and I got engaged, and I moved out of my apartment. Still, I took a picture of it, to remind me.

Anthropologie

The following items, all purchased from Anthropologie, are currently in my apartment:

An ornate white fake-porcelain cookie jar.
A ceramic berry crate that looks like a cardboard berry crate.
A gauzy sleeveless peach top covered in blue birds.
A floral lampshade.
A piece of metallic gold-colored fabric trim that was sold as a necklace.
A plaid asymmetrical dress that, whenever I wear it, other women always ask, "Where did you get that?" and then I say, "I got it at Anthropologie," and then they say "Ohmigod I love Anthropologie," and then I say, "Yeah, me, too." Often we have very little to say to each other afterward, but for that brief moment we understand each other.

I'm assuming you've been to an Anthropologie store (and I will confess that I'm secretly praying you're in one right now and you've picked up my book from one of their display tables, next to a stack of Tocca soaps, or perhaps a candle shaped like a finch), but just in case you haven't, or in case you are a guy, which means maybe you went in with your girlfriend or wife but didn't go past the couch at the front where you are supposed to sit and wait for her, Anthropologie is a retail chain that sells clothes, housewares, accessories, and gifts. But it's really so much more than that. It's an idea. A feeling.

Put simply: Every Anthropologie store feels like the manger in which Zooey Deschanel was born.

I'm obsessed with Anthropologie.

Part of the reason for the obsession has to do with where my shopping life began. My parents, who didn't have enough money to buy fancy expensive clothes and didn't have enough time to find decent affordable clothes, would take us shopping for just plain cheap clothes. My mom's primary store for me was one of the discount clothing shops on 14th Street in Manhattan that, to this day, is the reason I get a grim feeling when I walk down that block, something I avoid doing whenever possible.

It had the kind of fluorescent lighting that you see in a lot of low-budget stores, but there was something about this place that was especially soul-busting. The carpet was gray and dingy and always covered in random pins. All the clothes hung on circular metal racks, around which overworked moms would orbit as they picked through clothes, accompanied by the quick *click-click-click* noise of hanger hitting hanger. Their stereo system was always tuned to something like WPLJ, a station dedicated to awful radio remixes of techno songs that were bad to begin with.

I bought many terrible clothes there over the years, but one outfit stands out, mainly for the ratio of how rad I thought it was to how shit it really was. The top was a white short-sleeved blouse with a poppable collar that featured a yellowish illustration of kids playing on the beach, underneath which was written VAMOS A LA PLAYA! With this top, I would always, always, always wear a pair of tapered ankle-length yellow cotton pants. I thought I looked like a fun backup dancer in a Whitney Houston video (I didn't).

Sometime around the beginning of high school, I started to feel a pang that perhaps it was time to broaden my sartorial horizons. (I think it might have been the day I was wearing plaid green pants with an elastic waist and an XXL DIE YUPPIE SCUM T-shirt.) But I always struggled. Style is all about making a decision about what you want to project to everyone around you, and my self-esteem was too low for me to be interested in projecting much. That said, I went through a hippie phase, a metal phase (the most embarrassing one), then a grunge phase, then a modified grunge phase, and then I got out of college and bought a bunch of shit from the Gap so I could be a presentable temp.

Over time, I nurtured just the dimmest notion of how I

wanted to look. My example was the way my mom looked in photos from when I was a baby in the '70s. Comfortable and easygoing with a slight hipster/hippie edge, an occasional tassel hanging from a neckline, flared corduroy, thin floral tops, chunky jewelry she picked up when she was in the Peace Corps in Africa. This was my blueprint. But I didn't know how to do it. Then Anthropologie opened.

I don't remember exactly how old I was the first time I went in. But I know how it felt, because it feels the same way every single time, at every single store location. It's embarrassing how happy it makes me. I've never been a fourteen-year-old boy with an unwanted erection in the middle of math class, but that's kind of how I imagine it feels. Like my body is responding, in a humiliating but empirically biological way, to the amount of pressure this store is putting on the primordial pleasure center located deep within some cerebral coil. As soon as I see their faux-old barrel filled with faux-vintage glass doorknobs, or rest my eyes on a sweater with an embroidered kangaroo that has an actual pocket where the kangaroo's pocket is, I feel a sense of safety and inner peace. I feel prettier and girlier and a little thinner. I feel emotionally home. As if somewhere behind the rack of Eiffel Tower dish towels, I will find MY REAL DAD.

A few years ago someone at the *New York Times* wrote a "Critical Shopper" article about Anthropologie, offering up the theory that the store's décor is meant to evoke a nostalgia for a lost childhood home full of mementos and tchotchkes, the one inevitably sold after the parents' divorce. This rings true to me, even though my parents are still married, and still live in our childhood home, and our childhood home looks less like a magical Anthropologie store and more like if you stuffed all of Grey Gardens into a VW Bug.

But Anthropologie is selling more than just nostalgia. They're selling a fantasy about making yourself into a certain kind of girlfriend. The girlfriend you meet in the most magical places. You meet her at an outdoor market in Marrakesh where she is buying a little bell to hang in her window. Or maybe you're at a wine bar early on a Tuesday and she's the girl seated in the corner, in a kangaroo sweater, writing in her journal.

Once you start dating, she takes you back to her apartment, which is filled with mismatched teacups and green glass wine tumblers bought for a dollar a pop at an antiques store in the Hudson Valley. She has a dog-eared old copy of Julia Child's *Mastering the Art of French Cooking* and makes a perfect roast chicken filled with thyme. During dinner, she puts on music, some sort of folk pop, and when you ask her what you're listening to, she says, "Oh, my friend saw this band in Sweden, it's an import he burned for me, I don't think they record anymore…" Afterward, she'll serve you the madeleines she baked that morning in an apron patterned with dachshund silhouettes. This is the domestic version of the manic pixie dream girl.

When I think about this girl, and the twee garret where

she lives, she always feels like she could be someone's whole world, a complete and secret bubble in which everything refracts into a million colors and becomes more beautiful and alive, a little womb-space, lit, like Zooey Deschanel's bedroom in *500 Days of Summer*, with blue Christmas lights strung through her headboard.

I remember reading a quote from Ben Gibbard, the lead singer of Death Cab for Cutie, who used to be married to Zooey. He said, "I just remember when I met her I kept thinking, 'I can't believe this girl's even talking to me.'"

I've never had that. Every guy I've ever talked to has always totally been able to believe I am talking to him.

No matter how much I shop at Anthropologie, cherry-picking accents and baubles, knit hats and spangled Moroccan pillows, I know in my heart I can't truly be one of these girls. I will never strip naked in front of a lake and get some guy I just met to go skinny-dipping with me. I will never hand my headphones to Zach Braff and tell him that the band he's about to hear is guaranteed to change his life.

Types

One night, Mike and I were at a ridiculous event: a Lobster Roll Rumble. For three hours, twenty lobster shacks from the Northeast would sling their rolls for charity, and one would be dubbed the winner by us, the attendees. None of this is important to know, except for the fact that we were milling around with hundreds of other lobster roll aficionados when I saw my ex-boyfriend Tyler,[1] one of the worst men I have ever dated, which of course means at the time he was one of my favorites.

We hugged politely, and then I had the pleasure of introducing Tyler to my fiancé, making sure to articulate every syllable of the word—"This is my FEE-AHN-SAY." After we parted, Mike asked, "Who was that?" He was completely nonplussed when I told him that he'd met an ex (probably because he is a confident person, unlike

---

1   Name has not been changed.

me, who is undone by the notion that he ever had sex before meeting me).

His only comment on Tyler was "That guy is so completely your type."

"What do you mean?" I asked.

"You know," he replied. "Like a fat Jew."

It is true, I have a type. I have dated the same guy, more or less, for seventeen years. Not the same actual individual, but what are essentially Xeroxes of that individual. Mike is wrong in labeling the type "fat Jew," because that's not always been the case. Sometimes they're not fat, they're just doughy, and sometimes they just look like Jews despite being on Jesus's team. But I cannot deny that there is a look and a personality that calls to me. Let's dissect.

Appearance

- When it comes to facial hair, I am mad for a scruff. I will also horn up for full beards. In general, I like facial hair that would appear on an illustrated shepherd in a Haggadah. Anything that suggests someone who has just barely evolved past having paws gets my blood flowing.
- Body-type-wise, I would describe my sweet spot as someone who is trying a little bit to be in shape but is failing miserably. For example: I used to date a man (man-child) who, whenever we happened to wake up in the middle of the night, would suggest we get up

and eat Keebler Fudge Stripes Cookies while watching infomercials. It is embarrassing to admit that he later broke up with me. It's simply decimating to confess that we later dated again and he broke up with me again.

- Noses are of key importance. I need a large nose. Something with a bump. I cannot abide a small nose on anyone, really—men or women. I need the kind of nose that suggests some sort of Jewish/Italian/Greek/African influence. The kind of nose that says, "At some point in the history of my people, we were forced to flee."

- Sartorially, I like guys who wear T-shirts and old canvas sneakers and generally look like they are incapable of taking care of another human being.[2] My ideal partner looks like he was on the way to the Laundromat and got caught in a rainstorm, and then got drunk and fell asleep.

Celebrity inspiration: Mark Ruffalo, if he were a failure.

Lifestyle/Job/Personality

- Every guy I've ever dated is some kind of artist/writer, the type of guy who is talented and can do something interesting but then struggles to turn it into a meager living, which is fine with me, because I've never liked

---

2   I'm a comedy writer, so generally this is the only kind of man I meet anyway.

guys who make money. I don't know if it's the class issues I inherited from my father or some other masochistic impulse, but for most of my life, if a man was doing well, I didn't want any part of him. I liked guys who mumbled their charmingly unexpected jokes into their drinks, guys who made me laugh hysterically until the day they fucked up and then the hysterical laughing turned to hysterical crying.

• I always had a thing for awkward guys. Aw-shucksy guys who live in a flutter of papers and coins. Guys who seem shy and overwhelmed by the world. Manic pixie dream guys.

Celebrity inspiration: Jesse Eisenberg in the world's largest hooded sweatshirt.

With all my ex-boyfriends, I thought I was the only woman in the world who saw that they were attractive, who could find the desirability in their schnauzer noses and unkempt hair and bad jeans and scribbly jobs, who would take their hairy hands and translate their needs to the ungentle universe that couldn't possibly understand them. And with each of them, I was somehow always taken by surprise when it turned out that all their former lovers looked like Kirsten Dunst, and all their next girlfriends, the ones who would come right after me, looked like Carey Mulligan. It is one of the harshest realities of dating in New York that you can spy a man at a party who looks like a poor man's Woody Allen, start heading over to say hello, and then be cockblocked by his girlfriend, a woman who resembles but more likely simply just IS Scarlett Johansson.

So that is my type, this seemingly hapless but in fact completely capable, highly intelligent, but mind-elsewhere man. And what is it about this gestalt of hair and mumbling and Semitic looks? Why is this my type? This constellation of noses and T-shirts, shambling haircuts and web design jobs? Sometimes I wonder if it's genetic, if I had a great-great-grandmother who walked around Russia yearning for the most emotionally unavailable chubs in her shtetl. Or could it just be meaningless, like my love of bananas or my hatred of birds?

But I don't think so. My friends also have types. My friend Kayla has always been attracted to preppie, Waspy, khakied men in their mid-twenties. I have a male friend who fantasizes about curvy redheads. My friend Victoria is into men who would best be described as consistently horrible. With the distance that comes from me not actually being my friends, I'm able to see how in pursuing their type they are chasing some kind of ghost, haunted by a problem to which the type seems to be offering the solution. For most of my adult life, I did this as well. If insanity is, as they say, doing the same thing over and over again while expecting different results, then romantically I was batshit nuts.

Mike, my future husband, is not my type. He wears an expensive button-down collared shirt every day, including weekends. His haircut is corporate. He's an advertising executive. He is charming and funny, but he is not a mumbler. He's straightforward and clear. He does not pretend to need me as a go-between for him and the rest of the universe. He uses Molton Brown soap and spends $200 a week on dry cleaning, and I once saw him throw away a pair of Nike sneakers he'd owned for just five months because he thought they looked "ratty." (They did not.)

The only nod to my type is that he does have a fantastically large nose; but to clarify just how NOT my type he is, despite the presence of the large nose, no one ever thinks he's Jewish. They guess Irish. Which makes sense, because he's also pale. And his body isn't hairless exactly, but it doesn't have the sheep-like covering of wool that I'm used to.

In other words, he's nothing I thought I wanted. When we first started dating, I was confused. I would wake up in the morning and open my eyes and I'd have to wonder for a moment what this white businessman was doing asleep next to me. I'd stare at the back of his haircut, always recently refreshed into a kempt and conservative shape, and wonder why this person was here. I thought for sure he would be the exception that proved the rule and soon I'd return to some kind of hipster, sugar-addicted rabbinical school dropout. But then something happened:

I loved him.

And he loved me.

He loved me so much that I decided it was time for me to grow the fuck up and make him my new type.

The Bachelor

For years, I thought that only a certain kind of person watched *The Bachelor*. I assumed it was the kind of person whom I would loosely describe as part of "the problem," the problem being sexism, war, the death of culture, tackiness, babies having babies, and the general feeling that there isn't a surface left in America that a black light wouldn't reveal to be tainted with someone's shameful, Cheesecake Factory–laced DNA. But then one evening my friend Kate came over and we were drinking wine, and we wanted some TV to drink to, and it just so happened that the premiere episode of season 18 of *The Bachelor* was on. Hahaha, let's watch this as a joke, we said. And forty minutes later I realized I was feeling this warm, happy feeling, and when I took a moment to think about what it was, I had no other choice but to recognize that it was enjoyment. And not just a little of it. A tidal wave. And as soon as I started reaching out to see if anyone else I knew had experienced this sensation, I was surprised to find out how many respectable, hardworking, college-educated people, male and female, also are willing—desperate even—to talk about this ridiculous, incredible show.

Maybe it's because finding the right partner had been such an agonizing journey in my own life, but I feel a vicarious relief in seeing the process of picking a mate organized into a strict, codified structure. It's a comforting antidote to the modern neurosis in which we are all incapable of making a decision about whom we want to be with until we are out of time, i.e., dead.

The rhythm of the show is always the same. In the season premiere, we are introduced to our titular bachelor in a segment where he rambles about how desperately he wants to find The One. We then watch him exercise without his shirt on for a bit. After the commercial break, he stands outside the ~~polygamist compound~~ house and greets each of the bachelorettes as they arrive in black stretch limos (which you might think is cheesy, but be honest with yourself, being in a limo feels incredible and you know it).

The women on *The Bachelor* are a specific breed, and watching this season closely I grew fascinated with them. They are often from Atlanta, or the types of places that are defined by being next to other places, like Bakersfield, California. On some level they are the next phase in the life cycle of a stereotypical sorority girl, or conversely you could see them as just two phases away from becoming Real Housewives...but still, they are their own thing.

They are always shockingly pretty. And they always

have incredible bodies—all tawny flat stomachs peeking out of crop tops and perky tushes in white jeans. The characteristic that always impresses me most is that they all have a starkly defined tricep, outlined by a deeply chiseled shadow. This is a kind of bonus muscle that does not really appear in nature (on women anyway). I'm not totally sure how you get it, but my guess is it is only achievable through thousands of hours of precision toning. For me, it is the tricep that always gives away how hard these women are working at looking the way they do. But then, on top of all these enviable physical traits, they each spackle on entire Sephoras of makeup.

What the women do for a living is always a source of wonder. While many of them have the kinds of jobs you'd expect of twenty-three-year-olds—administrative assistant, legal assistant—there are always a few curveballs. There is a woman this season whose job is chyroned as "twin." Two seasons ago, one of the girls was a "Jumbotron operator," and in season 18 one of the women was always referred to as a "former NBA dancer." As in, her current job is having formerly danced for the NBA. Which makes me think that I should update my résumé to sell myself as a "future NBA dancer."

Personality-wise, they are all always nice, but a little bitchy, but mostly nice? And none of them—including the Bachelor—are ever funny. Not one person has ever made a joke in the entire history of the show. They occasionally laugh at stuff, but the source of this laughter is usually inexplicable.

Then there is the Bachelor himself. By all accounts, Juan Pablo, the Bachelor of season 18, was special. Juan Pablo is a former professional soccer player. He has a body that one could describe as "jacked," if one was interested in saying that word, and at first glance he is very handsome, until you've watched about four episodes and then you realize he looks like a mini horse. It's not so much because he's short, which he isn't, but rather just that the more he talks, the more you realize what a truly small human being he is. And it turned out that he was worse than just ridiculous; he was actually a genuine dick. The reveal of this dickishness, however, was a slow burn over the course of the season. It appeared first as a kind of boring sweetness, then morphed into a slightly shocking intellectual dullness, until in the final five episodes it became clear he was an anger management case.

His growing orneriness led to what was apparently the first semi-revolt in the history of the show, as starting in the middle of the episodic mating process, one bachelorette after another became disenchanted with him and left the show. Sometime around when Sharleen (the opera singer who displayed more self-awareness and intelligence than anyone on reality TV is ever asked to have) decided to leave, Mike, who'd been lingering around the edges of the couch whenever I watched the show, became fully addicted with me. Watching it together became, I am ashamed to say, the highlight of our week. We were both riveted by its inanity, but I got something more out of it:

If you want to know how a man really thinks, I truly believe one of the most instructive things you can do is to sit and watch *The Bachelor* with him. Because the women on the show seem more like fictional characters than real people, men feel free to talk about them in an unfiltered way they wouldn't use to talk about anyone you know, or even just women hypothetically.

For example: The runner-up in Juan Pablo's season was Clare, the tragic figure who had sex with him in the ocean, only to then be slut-shamed by him for "making him" have sex with her in the ocean. Clare was clearly a little crazy, although her decision to have sex with Juan Pablo was probably the sanest thing she did the entire season, since he turned out to not be good for much else. Her rival, Nikki, also seemed somewhat crazy, but in a way that was a little less dark than Clare.

When it came time for all of us to decide who would "win" (*us* being me, Juan Pablo, and Mike), we got into it. As crazy as I thought Clare was, she seemed like a nicer person than Nikki and should be Juan Pablo's choice. But then Mike informed me, "That's not how guys see her."

"What do you mean?" I asked innocently.

He hesitated, but for just a moment. "Clare seems like she'd be a good fuck," he said.

I was shocked to hear these words coming out of my husband's mouth; it was as if you one day heard your sweet domesticated King Charles spaniel call someone a vicious cunt. Of course I know men sometimes view women this way, but I didn't really understand what the specific signifiers of being a "good fuck" were, other than being hot and having a nice body, two qualities all the ladies had. What made Clare so special? I asked him to elaborate, and we got into a fight, and he told me I was being insecure, which I was outraged by...but it was the truth. I felt a pang realizing that of all the things I may have unintentionally radiated my whole life, "good fuck" was definitely not one of them. Maybe people can sometimes tell I'm a Leo?

The next morning I decided to double-check Mike's comments with my friend and co-worker Dan, a devoted husband and father of two who is one of the most polite and inherently decent men I know, and is one of those hyper-intelligent people who also happens to be obsessed with *The Bachelor*.

"Dan," I said, cornering him the moment he arrived at our office. "Do you see Clare as a good fuck?"

He looked panicked.

"Mike said so and I want to know what you think," I explained.

Reassured by the fact that Mike had said it first, he ventured slowly, "Um, I guess I know what he means."

"WHY WHAT IS IT ABOUT HER?" I unintentionally yelled at him.

"She just seems like the sort of person who is crazy enough to have no boundaries and would let you do anything," he said, looking around the room for a fire exit or accessible air shaft. "And also she has porn face."

I had to agree about the porn face.

Of course, I feel guilty watching this show. I feel guilty watching people cry and be upset for entertainment. My only defense is that I am never truly sure if these people are "real." Are they actors? Are they would-be actors? Or are they truly vulnerable human beings who are yearning for a relationship?

I have spent more time than I'm comfortable admitting pondering this question, and it bothers me that I can never be sure. Perhaps as a result of this desire for certainty, I have developed an elaborate fantasy of joining the show as a contestant myself, but in a very special *Bachelor* season where, instead of the usual tricep-ed, former-NBA-dancing, white-jeaned beauties, the entire roster of women is composed of women like me: Jewish girls with glasses in their thirties who went to liberal arts colleges.

My fantasy begins with our arrival at the house to meet "The" Bachelor. We each pull up in our big fancy limos, but instead of emerging bedecked in some kind of goddess evening gown, all of us are wearing big sweaters and Dansko clogs. And instead of greeting the Bachelor with big sexy hugs, every single one of us is awkward and offers a handshake while saying, "Can we all just acknowledge this is *so* nuts?"

Normally the dates on *The Bachelor* are all of an active variety—kayaking, or paintball, or some other physical thing where you could end up having sex by accident—but because every member of this new cast is constitutionally a delicate flower, different kinds of activities are in order. Such as:

On an early group date we all go on a CVS run to buy Advil. There are some laughs about who's choosing tablets over the gel capsules because they're smaller and easier to swallow.

Later on, as we are narrowed down to a smaller field, a sense of trust is established. A few of us ask the Bachelor if he will come glasses shopping with us. Several different stores are visited and many pairs are tried on before we decide to go with a frame very similar to our existing one.

There is the date where we go to a café and just talk about our dads.

There is the date where we go to the Met to see some important Chinese brush-painting exhibit that was written up in the *Times* and then eat at a terrible restaurant on the Upper East Side.

And at last, when the show has brought us down to two candidates, the final deciding date puts each of us—yes, I am one of the finalists—in the most intimate situation of all: watching all of the previous seasons of *The Bachelor* together.

This is the date that is the most important. This is how we will find out what he really thinks, and who he really is.

Connie

In the '60s, when he was putting himself through gradu-ate school, my father worked at Bellevue Hospital, where his job was to hold the heads of people receiving electroshock therapy. My dad was not in graduate school for anything related to medicine, psychology, hospitals, shock, or heads. He was getting his master's in English. Fifty years later, if you tell him you're going to therapy (something I would not recommend doing), he pictures you being strapped down by Nurse Ratched for the Cuckoo's Nest special. That's what he thinks all therapy is. Or maybe he pictures someone masquerading under the title "psychoanalyst" getting out of his chair to quietly grope you after he's put you into a trance with garbage lies about your parents.

But this isn't about my father. This is about me finding my way to therapy, way back in 2003, a couple of years after I had the spectacularly horrible split with Pete and every weakness that had been an ignorable little dripping faucet turned into a waterfall of low self-esteem, sadness, and anger. I paddled around in this muck for a year after we broke up, gradually getting worse, until I began to feel physically sick. My hands started tingling, I developed a numb patch on my cheek, and when I tried to type, my fingers were clumsy and missed the keys. I went on WebMD (THE RIGHT THING TO DO), where I found out that under no circumstances was I to believe anything other than the medically established true fact that I was dying of everything. In a panic, I ran to my primary care doctor at the time, Dr. Remy.

Dr. Remy was British, in his early fifties, with a chilly demeanor and more than a passing resemblance to William Hurt. I had a huge crush on him and would occasionally fantasize about an appointment with him touching my face and tracing the outline of my lips with his finger, and then gently kissing my forehead the way Mr. Darcy kisses Elizabeth in every decent adaptation of *Pride and Prejudice*.

Believe it or not, this never happened. However, his specialty was gastroenterology, and thus he believed the anus to be the oracle of health, the human equivalent of a dog's nose. This meant that every time I went to see him, regardless of the reason—a cold, a sore throat—he would put his finger in my butt. So in a way, it was like we were dating.

This time, I told him about the numb spot and tingling hands and my bad typing. As usual, he put his finger in my butt. He asked me if anything unusual was going on in my life, and I said no, not really, except for the breakup with my live-in boyfriend of six years. Before I even finished the sentence, he snapped off his plastic gloves and tossed them into the medical waste disposal, which is doctor sign language for "This appointment is over (you idiot)."

"You know when you go through a breakup, it's like going through a death," he said in his frosty accent. "You're depressed. Have you thought about speaking with someone?"

I hadn't. I'd thought about ripping open my gown and kissing him, but that was it.

I told him I'd consider it.

I know people whose parents sent them to therapy when they were seven and have never stopped going. In my therapy-averse household, the idea of "speaking to someone" had never come up.

I went to my company's HR department to get a copy of my insurance provider directory, which is one of the saddest things anyone can ever do, and in fact was so sad that the Internet was invented so no one would have to do it ever again.

Faced with a long list of random names and addresses, I tried to think about how to create preferences. I wanted to talk to a woman more than a man. I wanted a place close to my office so I could run out at lunch, be a fucking lunatic for an hour, and then run back. I noticed that most female therapists seemed to be named Linda, Debra, or Karen, so I figured I'd let them cancel each other out and I'd go with someone not named any of those things. I also remembered a piece of advice from my father, who once told me that you should choose a doctor based on the way their office answers the phone.

I started making calls. You'd be surprised how many therapists in Midtown then had very old answering machines, ones with actual tape where you hear it grinding on and then groaning off. I listened to their outgoing messages, and they all sounded the way my mom sounds on my parents' answering machine—like a hostage with a gun to her head, haltingly reciting a threat that will be broadcast on Al Jazeera. Only one person calmly and clearly stated her name and also mentioned that I should be aware that if I was on a cell phone, my message might not be transmitting. This struck me as a relatively sophisticated understanding of technology. I went ahead and made an appointment with this therapist, Connie, and then went back to crying at my desk.

Connie's office is in an old Midtown New York building, above a Pax. And it's always been the same. You walk past the security guard, who's kind enough to keep it to himself that he knows you're there because you're a train wreck, and then you always wait a bit too long for the elevator. Once in the elevator, you press 3 and then look at yourself in any of the four mirrors that line the walls, reflecting back at you an uncomfortably fragile, frizzy version of yourself. But you can't help but look forward to the moment you push the doorbell, and Connie buzzes you into the waiting room, where a white-noise machine purrs discreetly and there's a copy of *Architectural Digest* featuring a spread on Will and Jada Pinkett

Smith's Malibu mansion. You will sit and look at their home theater, and the surprising adobe theme, and you will think about what there is of significance to report about your own mansionless life.

Finally, some other patient opens Connie's door to leave and you pretend not to look at them even while you're trying to decide whether any of the details of their appearance give away that their problems might be more interesting than yours.

Then you rise and enter the inner sanctum, an office with buttery yellow walls and a painting of flowers and vases with some French words floating around the canvas, just to give the whole thing an air of sophistication. The room is warm and womb-like, and the only reminder of the real world is a window that looks across a gray alleyway and directly into a dentist's office, where sometimes, out of the corner of your eye, as you're talking about some particularly navel-gazing bullshit, you'll see someone in the middle of a root canal.

Finally, there is Connie herself, sitting in a big leather chair. She is always well dressed, often in a pantsuit with some chunky jewelry, a sort of free-spirited Hillary Clinton. She is now in her late sixties, with red hair and large owlish eyes magnified further by rectangular glasses that occasionally hang from a chain around her neck, the therapist's equivalent of a doctor's stethoscope.

The first time Connie and I met, I had the feeling I imagine an orphaned baby animal gets when it spots a female of another species and chooses to follow her around until she becomes its new mother, like the post-tsunami baby hippo that latched onto a matronly female tortoise. Connie grew up around the corner from where I grew up, albeit forty years earlier. She's Italian American, which means she understands food and crazy people, which means she's basically Jewish. Like the tortoise hippo mom, she reminds me of my mom, without actually being my mom.

In our first session, she asked me what had brought me to her office. I told her about Dr. Remy and about how the finger in the butt told him I needed therapy and was grieving a breakup. I talked about how betrayed I felt, and worse, how ugly I felt. She'd been listening and taking notes quietly until I said the ugly thing, at which point she looked up and said, "I don't understand the ugly thing. 'Cause I'm sitting over here and I feel like I'm looking at Audrey Hepburn."

There are a couple of things wrong with this. Number one, I do not remotely look like Audrey Hepburn. Nobody does. That's the whole point of Audrey Hepburn.

Number two, your therapist really shouldn't feel the need to give you an outrageously flattering compliment about your appearance to make you feel better. But she did anyway, and I started crying (I was crying a lot in those days). Partly because of the Hepburn thing but also because of an enormous sense of relief that I'd found someone I trusted. Or at least someone who was willing to accept money in exchange for never being exhausted by me.

Most therapists stick to a strict forty-five-minute clock. My sessions with Connie are an hour and fifteen minutes minimum. In the last few years, we have occasionally gabbed for upward of an hour and a half, if no one else is waiting. I'd like to think this is because she believes this is the amount of time it takes to have a productive session, but I know it's mostly her compensating for the fact that more often than not we spend at least twenty minutes talking about what happened last night on (over the years) *Sex and the City/Girls/Louie.* Earlier this year she and her husband went on a two-week trip to Iceland, and while she was away I had some very important bullshit happen in my relationship and I was really looking forward to getting her advice. When I showed up for my next appointment, I sat on the couch and politely asked her about her trip. She then spent the entire hour telling me about Iceland. How amazing it is, how beautiful and friendly the people are, how generous their system of government is when it comes to health insurance. I got up to go, and paid her an out-of-network fee of $150 for the travel recommendation.

A few weeks later I ran into my friend Greta, a college pal whom I sent to Connie about a year ago. Since then she's been nothing but effusive about how much she loves her. This time, however, after exchanging initial greetings, she gave me a look. "Did Connie talk to you about Iceland?"

So Connie doesn't always adhere to typical therapist protocol. But Connie has also healed me. When I walked into her office ten years ago—or was it eleven?—I was a broken eggshell. I didn't know what I was doing with my life. I was unmoored from the person who had been my person and I couldn't stop feeling the ache. I wept as I walked the ten blocks from the subway to my apartment every night. I was crushingly lonely. Once a week, I showed up to her office and sat cross-legged on her couch, often holding a pillow like a security blanket, as I dumped these feelings at her feet so she could do something about them. The horror over my ex being with someone younger, blonder, how it undid me to think about them together, how my idea of what love meant had drained away, leaving a cold white void, an empty sink in my gut. I told her about my obsessive Googling. This went on for months until one day, Connie leaned forward in her leather chair, brass bead necklace swinging forward, and told me, "Jess, you have a tape that's playing in your head. You need to decide to stop playing the tape." I stared into her eyes and pictured an old '80s cassette player. She was right.

We started going through my other tapes. The tape of my dad always pointing me toward the safest path in life, the path of plan B. The tape of me wanting to escape this path but not believing in myself. We started going through older tapes. Deep cuts.

It took years. But I gradually started to feel better. I started taking risks. I left my job and began my career. And I went on dates. Connie heard about all of them. There was the guy I brought in for one session of "couples therapy," at the end of which Connie said, "Well, you've been together a year, and this is supposed to be the honeymoon of a relationship, so just know it's only going to get harder from here." We broke up in the elevator on the way out.

There was the architect, a classic cad. When I told Connie he wore loafers without socks, she was agape. "Who is this phony?"

Years later, right before her daughter gave birth, Connie found out she needed foot surgery. We were supposed to do a phone session on a Wednesday night, and Connie was fifteen minutes late calling me, which was unusual for her. When she did, I could hear that she was scared. "I don't know how I'm going to help her," she said, her voice breaking.

"It's going to be okay," I said.

When I got engaged, I called my parents. They were thrilled, but even the happy news was not enough to break them of their habit of keeping every phone call as close to haiku-length as possible. I was on Martha's Vineyard with Mike, but I took a moment to email Connie a photo of us, captured two seconds after he gave me a ring in the middle of a wooded hike to the beach. Then we went to see a movie. When we emerged from the theater, I had a voicemail from Connie.

"Jessi," she began. "I'm watching the Olympics, and I don't even know what made me look at my iPad, but I did, and I see you and this ring, and I'm shaking. I'm shaking."

The message goes on for seven minutes. She seems to be signing off about ten different times, but then launches into another torrent of well wishes. "You just take real good care of each other," she said. "Real good."

I still haven't deleted it.

When I returned from the trip, I made an appointment to see her. I didn't have anything I needed to talk about, but she'd left me another message letting me know she had a gift for me. I went to her office, past the Pax and up the mirrored elevator, and then into the waiting room, where I looked at Jennifer Aniston's house in *Architectural Digest*.[1]

Once I was inside, Connie hugged me tightly. She looked at my finger and literally kissed the ring. Then she handed me a gift bag. Inside was a little jewelry box. "You need a place to put it when you do the dishes!" she said, and she was right. I did. After I thanked her for the gift, she gestured for me to sit down. "Tell me everything about the proposal." For a full out-of-network non-reimbursable hour, I gave her all the details.

---

1   A surprising amount of purple.

Carole King and the Saddest To-Do List Ever

When I was a little girl of about eight, I had this one very specific image of what it would look like to be a grown woman on my own. I am walking down Fifth Avenue in New York and I'm wearing a broad-brimmed hat, a full calf-length skirt and heels, white gloves, and big sunglasses. I'm carrying big fancy shopping bags in each hand. I am in control and living it up. Basically I am Julia Roberts in the second half of *Pretty Woman*.

About six years ago, when I was thirty-two and single and living in a somewhat shabby West Village apartment that Mike now calls "the lean-to," I realized I was staring at the beginning of a weekend where I had forgotten to make a single plan with anyone. *No problem*, I thought to myself, *I'll just take care of all the apartment stuff I've been neglecting*. I took out a notepad to make a list, because that is what women do: We make lists. After twenty minutes of hard thinking, I had two errands: "buy pillows" and "get new plants." Those were literally the *only* two things I had to do. Seeing these five horrifically lonely words in ink made me acutely aware of the possibility that if I were to die alone unexpectedly (a recurring fear), when the police went through my things they'd find this sad, pathetic list written by this pathetic, expired spinster. I pictured two of the older, more hardened cops kind of chuckling about it while a third cop, a younger rookie, would feel genuinely sad that this is how some ladies end up. Maybe he would even have to do the thing cops do on TV shows where they step outside to throw up.

I decided the only safe thing to do would be to circle the two things on my list, draw an arrow to the circle, and write "BIG PLANS" in as sarcastic a font as I could manage, so whoever found it would know that when I made this list, I was aware that it was unacceptably lame, and by signaling this awareness, the cops, or the neighbors who would smell my body, would know how cool and fun I actually had been. So I actually wrote the words "BIG PLANS," at which point the note transformed from a banal weekend agenda to a full-on transcript of a crazy person's conversation with herself.

I ended up going out to buy plants that needed to be potted. Because I don't know how to do anything that isn't the Internet, I called my friend Becky, who is the most self-reliant person I know. She grows her own vegetables; she has chickens; she is everything. She agreed to come over to help, and I started to feel like now the weekend was really cookin': potting plants, girlfriend heading over. This was being a strong awesome independent woman. I threw on Carole King's *Tapestry* so that as soon as Becky walked in, the festive party nature of our hang would be clear.

Ninety minutes later Becky and I were busy potting at my kitchen table. Just as I was placing my new fern (or whatever sad plant it was) into a ceramic pot, I somehow knocked the whole thing off the table and it broke into five pieces, its landing in no way softened by the huge amount of soil that was now all over my floor. Carole was mournfully singing "So Far Away." I looked at Becky and started to cry.

On *Sex and the City*, every now and then, they would include a short scene in which Carrie was alone in her apartment. She was always dressed a thousand times sexier than anyone would be dressed in their own home (or even how most people look going out, for that matter) and she was always perfectly content, either typing about the things that she couldn't help but wonder, or else happily reading and smoking by her window, a temperate breeze blowing first through a gauzy curtain and then through her fucking incredible hair. They never showed her just lying on her bed, staring into space while struggling to gather the will to think of something else to do. But as single people know, the real snapshots of living alone are often the most uncomfortable. The moments when you are shamefully eating a can of chocolate frosting for lunch (yup); the moments when you are scrolling through your phone, neurotically pressing REFRESH on all possible social apps to see if anyone has just now remembered they are in love with you; the moments when, if you were a part of a couple, your time would be filled with grocery shopping and brunch and bickering and sex; but since you are not, you sit frozen with anxiety on your couch as the clock seems to go in reverse.

There is a Zen saying that all men's miseries derive from not being able to sit in a quiet room alone. But it's hard to be Zen when you feel like your time in this quiet room might never end. When I was severely uncoupled—no boyfriend, no prospects, genuinely and deeply single—the need to fill time in a way that felt sexy and purposeful always seemed like a difficult homework assignment. On top of this, I often worked from home, which meant every day had the potential to turn into one long Bravo marathon. I wanted to structure a day where a hypothetical random snapshot of me looked like Carrie Bradshaw in her kimono, totally relaxed, not Brittany Murphy in *Girl, Interrupted*, diddling an old chicken under her bed. The key to doing this in a life devoid of the anchors that a spouse and kids usually provide is to build your day around tent-pole activities, things that will make you feel tethered to the calendar of humanity even though you are a single lonely alone person with no responsibilities.

When I lived by myself, these were mine:

6 a.m.—Wake up, be happy for two seconds, then remember every piercingly sad anxiety currently at play in my life. Get up to pee. Feel ever so slightly better for having peed. Try to go back to sleep.

9:15 a.m.—Go buy the *New York Times* from local head shop. Try to make friendly eye contact with the Arab guy at the register so he knows I'm not some typical American racist and that I like him and want to be friends. Always get rejected.

9:30 a.m.—Take the *Times* to my local café to read while eating my regular, balanced, healthy breakfast: scrambled egg whites with a mixed cup of blueberries and bananas on the side. Ordering the blueberries and bananas, instead of the normal fruit cup (which is chunks of hard melon and cantaloupe), is part of a fraught negotiation with the painfully adorable girls behind the counter, who always look confused. Explain that this has been done for me in the past. Get annoyed that this conversation has to be repeated every day but realize it takes up more time so it's not actually that bad. Once settled at my table with my paper and my food, take a moment to appreciate the peacefulness at this quaint old place.[1]

10:30 a.m.–12:15 p.m.—Return home. Sit down and try to write something. Look at everyone I've ever dated on Facebook and also join LinkedIn just to look at them on LinkedIn. Proceed to receive hundreds of LinkedIn re-

---

1   About a week after I wrote these words, I found out that one of the regulars of this café, a man I sat next to many times a week for years, had murdered his wife with an ax in their home.

quests a month for the rest of my life, never figure out how to get off LinkedIn.

12:30–1:30 p.m.—Lunchtime. My lunch is spinach-and-cheese ravioli with two glasses of white wine. Boil the ravioli and also heat up a store-bought artisanal tomato sauce to feel like I am really a home cook, like Julia Child. Turn on the DVR'd episode of that morning's *The View* to watch Hot Topics.

1:30 p.m.–4 p.m.—Lose steam on writing. Eat two dainty squares of a Ritter dark chocolate bar that feels a little fancy, put the bar back in the fridge, sit down as if to stop eating it, get up again, and then gobble the whole thing.

4 p.m.—*Oprah* time. I was devastated when *Oprah* ended. For years, watching *Oprah* was my closing tent pole of the day. No matter how badly I'd written, no matter what I'd failed to complete, as long as I tried to work until four, that was a day I'd shown up. And the reward was watching Oprah talk to sex addicts or sad moms or Jane Fonda for an hour, during which I'd have another glass or two of wine and know that I could now downshift into evening and figure out who I would call to go get a drunkish dinner.

Together, these activities gave my day a shape, a journey from waking to sleep. But that journey was always fraught with the idea that I should be having more fun somehow. One night me and my three single girlfriends decided we should go out. We spent probably about forty-five minutes total reassuring one another we were just a group of friends getting some drinks and food, and we were *not* having a Girls' Night Out, because Girls' Night Out is a cliché and it's embarrassing. On our way to dinner we ran into a handsome male friend of mine whom we all had a secret crush on. We stopped to chat.

After exchanging hellos, he looked me up and down and said, "Nice girls' night out shirt."

He was trying to be nice. And in fairness to him, I was wearing a gold sequin tank top. But his comment highlighted the problem when you are single: No matter what you are doing, there is always the danger of looking exactly like the kind of person you are trying not to look like.

The question, then, is whom do you aim to look like, in this tenuous world of being an unmarried, unboyfriended woman? How can you look, when you are alone in your house, like you are not trying too hard, or neurotically frozen, or called out by strangers for your glitter top, or crying to Carole King at home as you scrape a fern off your floorboards?

Ironically, maybe the answer is Carole King.

I have always been obsessed with the picture of her on the cover of *Tapestry*. It's one of those iconic 1970s lady photos, of Carole barefoot in bell-bottoms and a shmata blouse and frizzy Jew hair, seated in a window, in front of a patterned hippie curtain, with her cat at her feet. She seems content; not overjoyed, not sad, just…fine. She's not self-conscious, and she's not letting us stare at her without meeting our gaze. She definitely doesn't give a shit what we think of her outfit, or the fact that she's by herself. She doesn't give a shit because she wrote "Natural Woman," and "Will You Still Love Me Tomorrow," and "You've Got a Friend," and "It's Too Late," and "I Feel the Earth Move," and hundreds of other masterpieces. She's a badass. She can have as many fucking cats as she wants.

The Lingerie Dilemma

I have never known what I'm supposed to do about underwear. I'm saying *underwear* because I don't like the word *lingerie*. "Lingerie" seems to exist solely to make you feel bad about yourself if you're still just wearing "underwear." (Poodles wear lingerie. Wolves wear underwear.) I understand lingerie even less than I understand underwear, but what I'm saying is I fundamentally don't understand either. Add to the equation the question of what men want me to do re: my underwear, and the fog gets even thicker. And lastly, if you want to know what *I* want men to want when it comes to my underwear, I have no idea anymore. I want to be sexy and comfortable and I want men to want to unwrap me like I'm a Christmas gift, but I also want to be left alone and take a nap.

The whole thing is a massive tangle for which I place a large degree of blame on the Victoria's Secret catalog, an insidious publication that has inevitably shown up at every address I've ever been attached to, no matter how much I don't want it and have expressly put it out into the universe that I would like to never see it again. Does anyone know how to make this thing go away? Do the Obamas get a Victoria's Secret catalog at the White House still addressed to "Jimmy Carter or Current Resident"? I've made every effort and still, once a month, I open my mailbox to find it curled up and waiting for me like a snake.

I always almost throw it out and then I take a quick look at the tawny scrawny lion-maned lady on the cover, her perfect boobs hovering perfectly in their Angelic™ sling, and I think, *Well, maybe I should just check in.* And then I drop it in the magazine rack next to my toilet and the next time I am in the bathroom,[1] I start thumbing through and, page by decimating page, get the sinking feeling that I should be disqualified from being considered a female, if that hasn't happened already.

Victoria's Secret sets the standard for what underwear is supposed to look like. According to them, no woman should ever leave the house without wearing a matching bra and underwear set that is, at the very least, sexy enough for a fifteen-year-old boy to jerk off to. There is nothing in their catalog that sanctions what I do, which is to wear the same six pairs of basic Gap underwear in rotation for years until they start to resemble tattered old pirate flags.

Victoria's Secret's advertising is so ubiquitous, and their brand so vividly marketed, that if you live in the

---

1   Shitting.

United States at least, it's abundantly clear what they think you should look like when you take off your clothes, even when there's no one else around and you're just home alone making a peanut butter sandwich. It's also clear they don't want you to be eating a peanut butter sandwich.

But before my idea of what underwear was supposed to be was informed by the thong-industrial complex, I was a little girl. My underwear came in three-packs, sealed in plastic bags that hung on hooks at CVS or Duane Reade. (I continued to buy underwear this way into my twenties.) I was severely flat-chested even after reaching the age when puberty normally begins, so when it came to bras, I knew nothing. Around the seventh grade, a group of boys began sidling up to the girls, draping their arms around their necks, and rubbing their fingers along our shoulders. They would make bullshit conversation while not-so-subtly feeling for a strap. In this ingenious manner, they discovered who was wearing a bra and who was not. I was not. If you are wondering if it was cooler to be on the wearing or not wearing a bra list, it was one million times cooler to be wearing a bra. Even though I absolutely didn't need one, I began to feel like unless I owned a bra, I was somehow only a girl on a technicality.

I didn't even fully understand what a bra was for; what inherent mechanical problem breasts posed for which bras offered a solution. Part of this was because I rarely saw my mother's bras. My mother is tall and very lithe, so her bra needs were not vast. She wasn't one of those ladies from a Tennessee Williams film adaptation who has her bras perched to dry on a shower rod like rare birds, or flung dramatically around a couch. A bra appearance was like the fleeting sight of a mouse in the house. She had maybe three of them and they were all plain white cotton.

At home alone after school one day, I dug through my mom's drawers until I found a bra. After creating a cat's cradle out of it for the better part of an hour, I finally wrangled myself into it correctly. I wanted to gaze at myself to see if I was now a sexual being. Unfortunately, we did not have a full-length mirror, so I went into our bathroom in just the bra and my purchased-in-a-bag underwear, climbed up on the side of the tub, held on to the shower curtain rod, and leaned toward the medicine cabinet mirror, trying to strike a sexy pose. I didn't look sexy. I looked like someone trying to escape from a storm drain.

But what I remember most vividly, despite the reality of how pathetic I looked, is that I suddenly *felt* sexy. Even though the bra (which was very small) was too big, for the first time I had the sensation of feeling as if I had *the potential* to have breasts. Wanting to push my pinup look farther, I decided to try rolling up the sides of my underwear (there were significant sides) to create more of a "string bikini" effect. It didn't work. It didn't matter.

It was the first time I looked in the mirror and *wanted* something from what I was seeing.

I wanted to look like a Sexy Lady.

Either my mother noticed that I'd rummaged through

her bras, or else maybe I was beginning to have some pre-adolescent floppage, because one weekend she announced that it was time to take me to get my very own bra. I was excited. I pictured visiting a dream-like feminine space where I would go on an intimate journey of bra discovery and feel sexual and womanly and wouldn't the boys in my seventh-grade class be surprised when they reached around my shoulder again and felt the telltale sign that I was now a sexually alluring sex woman.

I pictured bra shopping this way because I hadn't yet been introduced to the concept of bra ladies. I didn't know that getting a bra, especially your first bra, most often involves standing topless in front of a slightly cranky Jewish/Russian woman of a certain age who isn't happy to see you or your tiny tits, who then takes out an ancient tape measure that always has the same color and texture as the original Constitution and wraps it around your torso.

My mother took me to a store on 8th Street called Lee Baumann, which was less a feminine fantasy space than a warren of plastic bins and old cardboard boxes filled with utilitarian bras that you would most definitely not see on the cover of Victoria's Secret. I remember the woman who measured me had that hair color that only a certain kind of old lady has, a kind of unnatural pink-brown, and if she noticed my shyness about taking my shirt off in front of her she did not say or do anything to put me at ease.

The whole experience was horribly embarrassing, but

I did leave with maybe two bras, both the color of Band-Aids, and I felt triumphant. I was now strapped in, ready for…whatever happens when you wear a bra that resembles a medical-grade compression stocking.

Nothing happened.

I didn't have a boyfriend until I was nineteen. He was almost as virginal as I was, which meant sexy underwear wasn't required for him to get excited. Still, my primitive understanding of how humans have sex meant that he was supposed to want to see me in lingerie. At each holiday and birthday, I expected him to gift me with some kind of naughtily wrapped box, but it never happened. He did buy me an electric foot massaging plate from one of those open storefronts on Canal Street, and I also recall a top from H&M that had the price tag hanging off it.[2]

In our second or third year together, I recall insisting that he buy me lingerie. Because there is nothing sexier than receiving sexy underthings that you have DEMANDED of another person. The result of this request was a white satiny slip thing that he presented with the dutiful obedience of a cat leaving a dead mouse at your bedroom door. It was the most virginal version of sexy underwear imaginable. It was loose and was at least a size too big. At best, it could be described as sweetly unflattering.

Still, in my mind, it checked off an important relationship box: My boyfriend had bought me lingerie. I

---

2   Nine bucks.

remember putting it on for the first time and waiting for him to get some kind of super-intense steroidal erection in response to the exotically attired temptress before him. I don't remember exactly what happened, but I know it wasn't that. If anything, when I think back to that relationship now, I mainly remember us watching Mets games and eating spinachy Indian food.

When we broke up after six years, I found myself single for the first time as an adult. I felt ill prepared. At some point in that relationship, I had upgraded from regular Hanes-in-a-bag underwear to their "bikini" line, which still came in a bag but had a higher-cut leg on the sides. It was more breathable than sultry. I figured if I was going to be Hot to Trot™ in the Big City™ it was time to step up my underwear game. I didn't actually think in those exact words; it was more like I just felt lonely and sad and isolated and was flailing for a way to feel attractive again. But Hot to Trot in the Big City sounds better.

So I made my way to Victoria's Secret on my own. Even though I was now in my mid-twenties, I still harbored a bit of my lingerie-shopping fantasy from when I was a kid, that I would walk into Victoria's Secret and transform into a tawny scrawny lioness like those ladies on the catalog with the wings and the smiles and the brond hair.

That is not what happens at Victoria's Secret.

Victoria's real secret, or at least it was a secret to me, is that their stores are shitshows.

The first thing that strikes you when you walk into a

Victoria's Secret is the color of the walls, which are an aggressive, relentless pink. I suppose the purpose of this is to reinforce an atmosphere of undeniable femininity, but instead I always feel like I'm walking into someone else's vagina. And not just any old vagina, but one that employs an army of women in inexplicably mannish black suits. Unlike the bra fitters at Lee Baumann, who exude the toughness of a people who've escaped the Cossacks, these ladies, in their corporate attire, look and act more like bank tellers in a land where the economy is tits and the currency is demarked in the cup sizes A, B, C, and D. Their main task is rifling through little drawers under the display cases for your size. The little drawers seem to be unlocked, and you could rifle through them yourself, but it seems to be understood that you mustn't do this. I don't know what would happen if you did. But you mustn't.

The second thing you notice is that the tawny scrawny lionesses from their ads do not seem to shop there. Instead, I am there, along with an average assortment of deer and mice and hippos—none of us tawny, most of us pasty.

And more often than not, their bras and underwear, which seem in their campaigns to have been beamed down from a planet that's thinner and more precious than ours, are carelessly stuffed into sale baskets. We ~~wildebeests~~ patrons, yearning to be Sexy™, crowd around and elbow each other for $5 thongs sadly tangled into ratking-level knots.

Often these buckets contain deals that are shockingly, almost disturbingly, generous, i.e., fifteen pairs of string bikinis for $4; the kinds of prices that serve to remind you that the "panty" you're hoping will make you Alluring™ was probably assembled by an underpaid, potentially underage, laborer™ in the third™ world™.[3]

Still, like the rest of the hopeful ~~bison~~ shoppers, I would leave Victoria's Secret with an embarrassingly pink bag, filled with optimism that what I'd purchased there would turn me into a ~~fuckstick~~ Angel™. I remember one of the first things I bought there was a pair of red bikini underwear that had the store's name on the waistband. I had never owned a pair of red underwear before, and putting them in my drawer that night I felt like a slutty little nymph (in the best way). I wore them to work the next day, and it wasn't long before I was attracting male attention. It should be noted that the male attention I received was only from a friendly married co-worker who beckoned me into his office and then, embarrassed, whispered into my ear that my underwear had bunched way up over the top of my pants in the back and I might want to tug them down.[4]

Was any of this agita worth the bother?

Over the years, I would ask boyfriends if they cared

---

3 I'm just kidding around. I'm sure Victoria's Secret would never exploit anyone. Right? I mean, of course they wouldn't. Would they? They seem very against exploiting anyone. Well, maybe they exploit women's bodies in their advertising a little bit. Just kidding; everything's fine with them. Is it? I'm hungry.

4 Thank you, Richard!

about lingerie, and the answer was always no. Their standard explanation was that for men, nothing is as exciting as getting all of a woman's clothes off, and fancy underthings are simply a speed bump in the way of that goal. But I never believed them. How can there be a gadillion-dollar industry around tricked-out lady underwear if there aren't gadillions of men demanding it? It doesn't seem possible.

What began to bother me the most was the idea that they were lying, that they all loved lingerie—and they simply didn't want to see ME in lingerie. This irritating little burr of an idea grew into a full-fledged paranoia. I worried that me trying to wear expensive underwear had the same visual effect as William Wegman's photographs of his Weimaraner dressed as a chef—comic, jarring, slightly repulsive.

This fear continued to gnaw at me until the spring of 2007, when for the first time in my life I had an affair. Not an affair like a married affair, but an affair like the kind of affair where you meet someone from another country who's in town for just a few weeks, and in that short amount of time you decide you are maybe in love with them, and after days of long walks and showing them where you went to elementary school, you kiss on a New York City sidewalk at two in the morning. The whole thing was short and intense, unlike most of my relationships in the years leading up to it, which had tended to be long and dull.

Of course, I couldn't quit while I was ahead, which led

to me flying to Europe on New Year's Eve, using every single one of my frequent flier miles. A few weeks after I returned, in the midst of a busy work/travel schedule, he offered to come visit me for the forty-eight hours he would be free in the next four months. Excited that this might be the beginning of my relationship with my Husband, I decided the occasion called for a serious lingerie attempt, with no bullshitting around at Victoria's Secret, which I'd finally realized was the McDonald's of underwear stores.

This is how I found myself at La Petite Coquette, a lingerie store in Greenwich Village. I'd passed it a million times over the years, noting their carefully curated store window display for Valentine's Day (theme = Frisky). Their displays for every holiday looked sort of the same, i.e., Frisky Christmas, Frisky Easter, etc. Their inventory appeared classier than the offerings at VS (no panties with JUICY or SKANK on the butt), so on the day before my man friend's arrival I walked over.

That morning I'd started to feel the first little inkling of a cold coming on. This often happens to me in the week leading up to an event that might bring some kind of joy. My body rejects this foreign feeling and crashes. But I was determined not to miss out on a visit from my gentleman caller, so I took some echinacea and decided I would fight it off.

I had always assumed that La Petite Coquette was French in name only, but it turned out the three women who worked there were in fact real French ladies from actual France, which meant they were impossibly thin and beautiful in that French off-kilter jolie-laide way. They all basically looked like Charlotte Gainsbourg.

One of the Charlottes floated over to me and asked if I was looking for anything in particular. I was actually prepared with an answer, having thought about what lingerie identity I could plausibly pull off. I'd decided I could try a matching chemise and underwear set (I just had to Google "chemise" to make sure that's what it's called). If you are a man, or a woman who doesn't waste her time with this nonsense, a chemise is basically a loose long top that covers your butt, yet can flash a solid amount of boob. When I explained this to Charlotte #1, she said she would pull a few things for me and ushered me into a fitting space, the kind where there's a curtain that's not nearly big enough to actually give you privacy. (I don't know why so many stores have this issue. It's very obvious it's a problem and yet the clerks always pretend like they're not seeing your nips or peen or whatever is clearly visible through the gapingly open margins of their fitting rooms.) She asked me what size underwear she should bring. I said medium or large, but she didn't hear me and asked me to repeat myself. "MEDIUM OR LARGE." I really wasn't feeling well.

She brought back a selection of gauzy little outfits, all of which were paired with thongs as the bottom half. "Do you have any sets that aren't thongs?" I asked. She looked at me like I was asking if she would like to join ISIS. They did not. I closed the curtain and put on the medium thong. I looked like a groundhog wearing a tiny belt. I tried on the large thong, which yielded results that were only slightly better. I then endured the indignity of having to yell back over the curtain that I needed the thong in an extra large. She couldn't seem to fathom that such a size even existed. I could feel my temperature climbing. I was definitely getting the flu. I suddenly found myself missing Victoria's Secret and their drawers full of underwear that go up to size infinity.

We went back and forth this way for an hour, during which my physical condition continued to deteriorate. Charlotte kept returning to my dressing room with lacy little trifles that did not fit me. By the time she handed me a scalloped black thong with the promise, "Duhn't wehrrree [French pronunciation of *worry*], theez run very large," I was sopping in sweat. I tried on the thong that ran very large to find that it still barely fit. This was actually the least distressing thing that was happening, because as it turns out, I had started to cry.

I was crying because, just like when I was a little girl, I sorely wanted something from my reflection that I wasn't getting. I wanted to be desired. I wanted to be desired the way women are desired in movies and commercials and Victoria's Secret catalogs and all that cheesy shit. Because looking good in lingerie felt like part of the package of being female. And to be female means to inspire *lust*. And lust seemed inextricably snarled with G-strings and bralettes and demicups and garters.

Weeping and sweating in a dressing room, on the other hand, felt like the opposite of lust.

I left La Petite Coquette with the black scalloped thong, which only kind of fit, and its matching bra and chemise counterpart. I was a mess. At home I got into bed with a mug of tea, but not before I took my lingerie arsenal and carefully folded the pieces into my underwear drawer, where they looked like purebred French poodles sleeping with a pack of mutts (i.e., stretched-out Gap boy shorts).

On the first night of my Affair's stay, I was excited for him to take off my clothes and reveal the $375 investment I'd made in our sex life.

But all I remember when I think back to that night is how dark it was in my room; that the underwear was revealed with no reaction or commentary; that the underwear itself was off in seconds and ended up on the floor. I don't remember anything about the sex itself. I remember that in the two days we were together, my sense that he was my Husband began to fade. He was jet-lagged, and always seemed a little distracted. The magic of our initial rendezvous had been replaced by a low-grade anxiety that seemed to constantly buzz between us like AM radio static. I remember I had bought tulips, and that at one point he walked naked through my apartment with the stem of one of the tulips tucked into his butt cheeks to make me laugh, and I remember that he wanted to make me laugh because I was sad. I remember I was sad because I realized he did not feel the same way about me that I did about him.

There is that Maya Angelou quote about how people may forget what you said or what you did, but they will never forget how you made them feel. I don't remember the last words that guy and I said to each other.

But I remember feeling that lingerie is really never worth the agita.

How to Get Engaged

It's about ten thirty a.m. and I am sitting at a bar at Logan Airport (Boston Beer Works, specifically), sucking down my third giant glass of lager. I'm a little enamored of the bartender, a solidly built young woman whose working-class accent hovers somewhere between Ben Affleck in *Good Will Hunting* and Mark Wahlberg in *The Departed*. I have always found this accent endearing. My boyfriend Mike grew up in Boston but he doesn't speak with the accent, which is yet another reason that right now he is a massive disappointment. He is the reason I am here, waiting for a puddle-jumper Cape Air flight to Martha's Vineyard, where I am going to meet my friends Jenny and Zander.[1]

They will comfort me about the fact that I wasn't supposed to be there. I was supposed to be in Los Angeles,

---

1   They're in the middle of a five-day stay in the guesthouse of Rose Styron, William Styron's widow, the result of Jenny winning a charity auction for the *Paris Review*.

doing a victory circle around the city as friends congratulated Mike and me on getting engaged. That is no longer happening now. What is happening now is that I am guzzling beer for breakfast, and very quickly I am drunk. Among other things, I'm trying to get over the fact that when I checked in for my flight, the clerk asked me for my weight, which at first I thought was a joke. But that's how small this plane is. If my butt's too big, we could die. Thinking about this possibility, as well as the fact that the man whom I thought I was spending the rest of my life with just choked on proposing to me, has led me to the third beer. I am tilting toward very drunk as I start messaging all my girlfriends to tell them where I am and what has happened. Over the next few days, as they begin to respond, via text, email, and phone, I will be initiated into an ancient world of female knowledge, one that I never thought I'd have to know, about how men and women really decide to get engaged.

Mike and I were set up on a blind date, analog-style—as in we were actually set up by a mutual friend, not the Internet. We had a slow start, but once we began to date in earnest, there never seemed to be any real doubt that we would be together forever. This was the inverse of most other serious relationships I'd been in in my thirties, in which the breakup had always been taken as the assumption. (Seriously, my last boyfriend before Mike—a man I'd dated TWICE, like a big fat dummy—was begging me to spend Thanksgiving with his family about an hour and a half before we went back to my house, where, after some gentle prodding, he admitted he wanted to break up.)

But that wasn't Mike and me. Two months in, before he even told me he loved me, we were enjoying a long Labor Day weekend—picnicking on the rug in his apartment, drinking whiskey, and talking about where we were on 9/11 (the deepest conversation you can have with another person). I told him I knew we'd been spending so much time together because he'd had the week off from work, and he shouldn't feel any pressure to continue this schedule because I was aware we'd been in a bit of a bubble.

He looked out the window, and then at me, and said, "But the thing is, I'm in."

I'm in.

Every girlfriend I told that story to—and I told all of them—had the same reaction. Their eyes would well up and they'd softly whisper, "Oh my God."

So that's how it was.

From "I'm in" onward, Mike was never scared of commitment. After six months, he started asking if I wanted to move in with him. Part of me did,[2] but part of me also knew what a shitshow it would be to move out again if things fell apart,[3] and part of me also kept thinking about the lyrics to "Single Ladies," and I thought if Beyoncé was saying he should put a ring on it I should probably listen, because just fucking look at her.

---

2   His apartment was awesome.
3   Flashback to me finding lube bottle in ex's apartment.

But I wasn't stressed about getting engaged. My worst nightmare—worse even than my childhood nightmare about being abducted by Alf—was one day having to cajole or bully a guy into marrying me by giving him an ultimatum. In my head, that was a move reserved for a certain type of woman who was not me, and I'm not exactly sure how to describe her, but in a movie she would be played by Jeanne Tripplehorn carrying a big expensive purse and yelling into a very large cell phone.

In late 2011, we started talking in earnest about the idea that we would get married. I didn't care how he proposed, and I didn't especially care when he did it, just that he wanted to do it. Which I knew he did. Because he'd told me. Did I mention we had gone to couples therapy to work out some issues? Whatever, doesn't matter. He wanted to do it. Right? We'd have these little shorthand conversations—

"So, just checking, just so I know, because I'm not Jeanne Tripplehorn on a large cell phone, when?"

Mike said February of next year, after we've worked on our issues a little while longer.

Cool! My life is all set! It's so nice when your life is going perfectly.

Not only did I feel sure this engagement would happen, so did everyone else. Starting about a year into our relationship, every time I told anyone we were going on any kind of vacation they would get a look in their eyes and whisper, "You're getting engaged, right?" This speculation hit a fever pitch right before our trip to Paris for his fortieth birthday. I'm not sure if Parisians are aware of this, but in the minds of many Americans, their museums, rich history, and incredible food are all a backdrop for American men to fork over little blue boxes to the American women who have ensnared them.

But we did not get engaged in Paris. Nor did we get engaged in Turks and Caicos, nor on our trip to various quaint spas in the Northeast.

Then "February of next year" arrives. Mike has been promoted, and this is the first year he is in charge of a very important yearly work event. He is stressed out. I know he's stressed out, but he needs me to know it's really bad, worse than I can imagine. I tell him I know it's bad and I am supportive! He says he can't deal with getting engaged until after the event, which is in the middle of March. I am an angel-saint, so I say this is fine, I don't care. I click, for maybe a millimeter of a second, on some engagement rings online before shamefully slamming my laptop closed, albeit with a little grin on my face. It's amazing how calm I am about my own life!

So we start planning a vacation for after his work event, a vacation he'll especially need after working so hard. But it's also perfect, because it's when we're going to get engaged. He asks where I want to go, and I say I've always dreamed of going to Napa, something I've never done before. He's never been to Big Sur, so we split the difference and talk about flying to San Francisco, driving to Napa for a few days, then continuing on to Big Sur. Mike, who has a decidedly luxe notion of vacationing, gets very excited about the idea of going to Post Ranch Inn, a hotel set on the cliffs of Northern California that has won every Most Luxurious, Most Ridiculous, Most Over the Top award from *Travel & Condé Whatever* magazine so many times in a row that now they're just showboating. The beauty and drama of it is so incredible that even visiting their website feels like a trip you cannot afford. The Spa at Post Ranch offers all kinds of California woo-woo services, including sessions of spiritual guidance billed as a "Drum Journey." I almost take the drum journey, but book a Reiki session instead, fearful that the drum journey could end in me leaving Big Sur with a bindi and a bong, the way some white chicks return from the Bahamas with cornrows.

So we book our spa appointments and make restaurant reservations in Napa and reserve a car. Our tickets home give us a layover in LA, where Mike has to be for a few days for work immediately after our vacation ends. I don't really have to be there but I figure I should go with him since we'll have just gotten engaged. I'll find stuff to do in between our Pinot-filled dinners with friends toasting us and asking have we thought about where we're doing it and we'll look at each other and smile because we know we're just going to enjoy being engaged for a while.

Then, the weekend before we leave for our trip, we get in a fight, and it spills over into the following week. It's nothing huge, but there's daily bickering, a low gaslight of negativity that is never totally extinguished. It's not the dream, to be at each other this way just before such an important moment in our shared lives, but here we are arguing in his car the morning before we're supposed to leave. As he's dropping me off at my apartment on his way in to work, I make him pull over for a moment so we can keep bitching at each other. After I lob another snipe into the air, Mike frowns and says, "Have you been so mad at me this week because you know I'm not proposing to you on this trip?"

!

... ...

Um, no.

I don't remember what exactly I had been mad about before that information came to light, because once that cat was out of the bag everything became kind of dark, as if someone had just dilated my pupils so that only one point was harshly clear while everything else was a smudge. I had to get out of the car, but the awkward part, the part that made this my life, was that my cleaning lady was working in my apartment, so I couldn't go home. I got out of the Toyota Matrix, while Mike yelled after me, and made my way to the one place that always felt safe: Spa Belles.[4]

Trying not to weep, I went inside to get a manicure and took a seat next to a girl who was waiting for a friend. A few minutes later, her friend walked in and

---

4   In case you're not familiar, Spa Belles is a chain of manicure places in New York City. They are usually pretty clean-ish. The dirtiest I ever saw one was after someone did a number two in the restroom and the toilet clogged, and I guess that someone was embarrassed and just ran off. (I was the someone.)

immediately raised her left hand, followed by the I-just-got-engaged scream. At which point her friend said, and these are her exact words: "Ohmigod! I knew something was up when he asked you to go to the top of the Empire State Building!"

Good grief.

I spent the day in a fog. I kept trying to make sense of how this could have happened, this misunderstanding. Was it a misunderstanding or a miscommunication? Or worse: Was this my wake-up call that I am one of those people who has no self-awareness? The type of human mosquito who clips her nails on an airplane or scream-talks into her cell phone at a café? I kept turning the situation over and over, trying to formulate an angle on the scenario that both made sense and wasn't decimating.

That evening, we started to pack. Our suitcases were open and we were silently folding clothes when I asked him, "So, are you not proposing on the trip because you wanted to propose in a different way, or because you're not sure you want to marry me?"

He was silent.

We spent the next three hours rotating between fighting, crying, drinking, talking, reasoning, and threatening. At one point I panicked and said I had to get out of the house. I stood up to grab my stuff, whereupon Mike panicked and grabbed my arm and started weeping. It was like a soap opera with a less talented, less attractive cast.

Whiskey came out. Some clothes made it into the bags, and then other clothes didn't go into bags, as he explained, over and over again, that he felt like we still had things to work out, that he didn't feel ready, that he just wasn't 100 percent sure, that maybe it could be a few more months, soon, just not now. I stared at little details of his bedroom, the ugly brown wool throw pillow with once white but now grayish embroidery, the even uglier white-noise machine perched quietly on top of the side table like a Band-Aid-colored beetle. I zeroed in on the checks of his shirt, looking at the blue check, then the white check. I was surprised at how many banal little objects were woven into this moment, and imagined they were all alive, and that all of them were as surprised as I was that the relationship was ending and that soon we'd all have to say good-bye forever.

I told him I didn't see the point of going on this insanely romantic trip anymore. I didn't want to go for a coastline horseback ride with some guy who didn't feel like he knew enough about me to marry me. You already know me, I insisted. I like dogs and comedy. I'm insecure but loving. That's who I am.

To make our seven a.m. flight, we were supposed to wake up at four thirty in the morning. From nine p.m. until three thirty in the morning, we debated over whether or not we should cancel the trip. At three forty-five a.m. we decided we would go, and fell asleep.

I woke up when the alarm went off, had one of those terrible moments of not remembering why I should be sad, and then groaned. We rode in total quiet to the airport, the little knot of anger behind my sternum getting tighter and tighter. As we were about to check ourselves in at the JetBlue kiosk, I hissed something jealous and miserable into his ear. Mike, furious, said we should turn around and leave. A little girl with a monkey backpack stared at us as we made a scene.

"What will I tell my parents?" I whimpered.

He pulled me over next to a bag drop, and we debated once again whether we would go on the trip. As we argued, the agent picked up my bag and put it on the conveyor belt.

We were going.

So we made it to San Francisco, where we'd planned to spend one night until leaving for Napa in the morning. On the plane, I'd promised Mike I would call a truce and suppress the negative feelings, but I was lying. At four in the afternoon, I walked into the hallway of our hotel and called my friend Kate, bawling. I couldn't do this. She offered to book me a flight home the next morning. I was a woman sobbing in a hotel corridor, which is kind of incredible, because when I was little I thought I was going to be a senator.

My spiral continued through what was supposed to have been our romantic dinner. I started sulking around appetizers, and a few glasses of (admittedly incredible) Sancerre later, I was yelling again. My tirade continued in the cab, in the elevator, up to our room, and even for a minute or two after Mike stormed out of our hotel room, because I wanted to make sure he heard me through the door.

I don't remember falling asleep. I woke up at dawn, and

Mike was next to me. He had returned to the room. I looked at the back of his neck, and felt three things, each crushing in its own way.

Exhaustion.

Love.

And uncertainty.

I knew I had two choices. Choice number one was that I could take Kate up on her offer and go home.

Choice number two was that I could continue on the trip with him, and most likely we'd be having that sad species of vacation couples go on when it's the last one they'll take together, and sometimes one person knows it and sometimes both people know it.

But I knew that if I left, our relationship would definitely be over, right now.

I touched his arm and said, "Let's go."

We wearily walked to pick up our rental car, and that is where a minor miracle occurred. They were sold out of the model we'd reserved, and so, at no extra cost, they upgraded us to a brand-new Volvo convertible with a leather interior the color of cream. When Mike turned on the engine, he gasped.

"Oh my God," he said. "The seats are heated."

The yuppie asshole in each of us was so in awe of the car that we both immediately cheered up and headed to wine country. (I did acknowledge it was only a minor miracle.)

The three days in Napa were a booze-soaked blur. We drank barrels of beautiful liquids and fell in love with our driver Tom, a gravel-voiced Vietnam vet with a passion for grapes. I focused on the pleasure of risotto and cheese, and we went to French Laundry, where I ate marrow. I forgot about being engaged, except for a dip in my heart every morning when I remembered I was on a bittersweet last vacation. I managed to pretend everything was fine.

Until we got to Big Sur and the Post Ranch Inn.

When you arrive at Post Ranch, the concierge hands you a glass of wine, which you will carry with you into the Lexus SUV used to shuttle you to the tree house where you will be staying. It has a fireplace and a hot tub and an outdoor tub and it's fucking nuts. A bellman shows you the location of the two cliff-side hot tubs, which overlook what looks like all of the Pacific Ocean at once. The concierge reminds you that if you want to use one of their Lexus convertibles, all you need to do is call the valet and it will be brought to your door, at any hour of the day or night. Yes, when you stay at Post Ranch you have free use of a Lexus. No one worries about a guest stealing a car, because why would anyone want to leave this place?

And it's only when we sit on one of the many little white stone benches scattered along the bluff that I feel tears coming again. Unlike the baloney that everyone believes about the inevitability of getting engaged in Paris, here it is not bullshit. Getting engaged is the reason this place exists. Who wouldn't think they were with their soul mate, even if it was a mistake, in a place like this? As we realized there were clouds rolling by BENEATH us, I could see Mike starting to feel just a bit sheepish about his decision not to propose here.

Over the next four days, I'd literally stew in the hot tubs; sometimes at dawn, sometimes at midnight. Here I was, a privileged speck soaking in one of the most awe-inspiring vistas in the world, and all I could do was text my friends about my relationship.

"This is what they do," my friend Tracy texted me. "This is his process." It was sunset, and I was sitting at the Post Ranch restaurant watching bats throw themselves against the huge floor-to-ceiling glass windows while Mike was in the bathroom.

"Help," I had written to Tracy, and to my friend Jessica, and to my friend Wendy.

Jessica wrote me back the next morning, as I was looking at a giant redwood tree, one of the most majestic living things in the world. "This is so fucked," she said. "Fuck him." Mike was up ahead, fiddling with his camera. "Has this ever happened to anyone else you know?" I thumb-typed.

"Yes," Jessica answered. "Literally every woman I know who's gotten married has gone through this bullshit before they got engaged." She went on to lay it down: "You need to not talk to him for a while. Don't be aggressive, he just needs to be scared you're leaving."

I said I thought this sounded like a game.

"Trust me," Jessica said.

I couldn't believe that I was suddenly ensnared in

the most humiliating relationship cliché of them all: the girlfriend giving an ultimatum. Jeanne Tripplehorn on the big cell phone, yelling at her dumb boyfriend to get his shit together.

Jenny texted me that Jessica was right. "This is just what guys do," she said.

On our third Post Ranch day, I went for my Reiki appointment. Although I was happy for the hour-long break from Mike, I was not expecting any more enlightenment than I would from a Magic 8 Ball. I was greeted in the waiting room by "Saja," who led me to the Reiki room, which was dark and filled with red and gold pillows and bronze bells.

She started the session by asking me if there was anything going on in my life I thought she might want to know about. I figured she probably didn't really want to know about any of it, so I simply told her I was having a hard week. She said I shouldn't expect to go into a trance or be hypnotized, but that at some point it might feel like I was dreaming. Whatever, Reiki lady. She rang a bell and started touching my back lightly; it wasn't massage, as she was just barely grazing my skin with her fingertips. For five minutes I lay on my stomach with my head in the face cradle, thinking bitterly about what a waste of money this was, and trying not to think about how much this room looked like the set of *Veronica's Closet*, until suddenly I felt like I was falling asleep. Except I knew I wasn't. My eyes were open but I had the sensation that I was watching a film, and that I was not in control of what was being projected in front of me. The movie began with me in the ocean, out in open water, and then I became aware of being born out of my mother's body. I met up with my first boyfriend, Pete, and we cried in each other's arms and I forgave him for hurting me. I had a cat whom I fed by spilling milk out of a teacup directly onto the tile floor, and then I was left standing in my kitchen holding an empty teacup and wondering who would fill it again. Every image seemed like an unsolvable equation that the next image would somehow solve. This series of pictures floated in front of me for what felt like days, although really it was about forty-five minutes.

Then Saja rang another bell, and I "woke up." I felt peaceful. We spoke about how I might want to try correcting the imbalances she'd felt between my masculine and feminine energy. I didn't know what this meant but it didn't matter, I loved Saja so much. I stumbled down the hallway toward the lobby, dizzy, but with a new understanding of the order of the universe. Everything made emotional sense.

And then I bumped into Rosie O'Donnell.

She was checking in for her massage or her Reiki session or maybe even her drum journey. She was wearing white jeans and a sweatshirt and sunglasses and her hair was a mess. It was like the polar bear from *Lost* had ambled into my childhood synagogue. What had, for a few tantalizing seconds, felt like a world in emotional order once again presented itself as unpredictable chaos. How was it possible that Rosie O'Donnell and I had both ended up in the same hippie spa in the middle of nowhere on this particular day? So many infinitesimally small decisions had to fall into place for us to cross paths. As I walked back to my glam tree house, occasionally hugging the side of the road to avoid a passing Lexus, I kept thinking about how the journey by which two people find each other and decide to make a life together must involve an accumulation of so many twists and turns for both. It's a mystery as to how it all gets done.

For instance: How did events align such that when I needed to get away from Mike, my two girlfriends happened to be on Martha's Vineyard in Rose Styron's guesthouse with an extra room available for me? How did these two awesome women happen to be on vacation at the very moment I needed them to get drunk with me till the wee hours and let me cry about how I was now, at thirty-seven, going to be single and starting over again? How was it that when I needed to write the most important letter of my life, telling him how profoundly disappointed I was and that I needed to move on, I was sitting in the same house where William Styron wrote *Sophie's Choice*?[5] What I'm really asking is, Why did it take all these things for me to be sitting here now, typing these words with a diamond ring on my left hand?

Because, as Mike later wrote to me, he was terrified.

---

5   To be clear: I am not comparing the letter I wrote to the novel *Sophie's Choice*. I'm just saying I was able to channel some Streep energy being in that room.

Because he was scared of repeating his parents' decimating divorce. Because he was sublimating lifelong fears of failing the way his father had.

But who knows the real answer? I don't.

I just know that what I learned is that this is often the way men and women decide to get engaged.

The Wedding Dress

A few days ago, Mike and I were eating key lime pie and watching *Say Yes to the Dress*. A bride-to-be was standing on a pedestal in an overly sequined dress, griping about a lack of "bling" and demanding to see another gown. We both chuckled about how silly she looked and how dumb it is to freak out over this trivial bullshit. But suddenly I remembered, mid-pie-bite, as some twenty-one-year-old from Atlanta was agreeing to be "jacked up" (this is *SYTTD* speak for allowing yourself to be accessorized—veil, jewelry, etc.—in order to prove to your skeptical mom that your dress makes you look like a classy bride and not a cheap common slutty slut), that just a few months ago *I was one of these ladies.*

Actually, that's not even true. I was, in fact, much worse.

The sad truth is: Over the spring and summer of 2013, I tried on over a hundred wedding dresses.

* * *

Immediately after we got engaged, friends and family started asking me what I was thinking about vis-à-vis a wedding dress. I gave everyone the same answer: "Oh, I'm not going to wear a wedding dress." And then, as I watched their eyes widen and their minds explode, I would feel this incredibly warm wave of self-satisfaction wash over me. It's very similar to the feeling I get when I tell people that while I understand that he may appeal to others, I do not personally find Brad Pitt attractive. No thanks, not for me!

We all enjoy the little moments when we can quietly announce to the world how special and unique we are; but the thing is, I genuinely didn't want to wear a wedding dress. I've simply never related to them. The poofiness, the taffeta-ness, the overall Cinderella-ness—none of it ever interested me. I've attended many weddings where I've watched a friend, someone I thought I knew well, walk down the aisle in an ensemble that rendered her essence somehow unrecognizable, like seeing your beloved pet Chihuahua in a neon Speedo. It's as if these dresses are designed to erase your individuality, leveling you into a universal symbol of femaleness, like that faceless woman wearing a triangle dress on the door of every ladies' restroom in America.

I didn't want to do that. My plan (as I elaborated to anyone who asked) was simply to spend "a little more than I normally would" on a festive but gorgeous but non-bridal dress. Maybe a Catherine Malandrino. A Zac

Posen. I'd identified a few designers I liked, but the common factor in all of my dress fantasies was how incredibly easy it would be for me, a humble feminist with almost no material needs, to accomplish this simple task.

What I wasn't expecting was the number of people who came out of the woodwork and actually volunteered to take me wedding dress shopping. A casual acquaintance, a woman I occasionally work with, lit up when I told her I was engaged. "Oooh," she said. "Are you going to go to Kleinfeld? If you are, could I go with you? I've always wanted to go." She lives in Chicago, but was willing to fly to New York to fulfill this lifelong dream.

Closer friends wanted to take me shopping as well. One friend, whom I had accompanied to a boutique to buy her wedding dress two years earlier, was quite eager to return the favor. "I'll make the appointment!" she offered. I didn't know you had to make an appointment to go dress shopping. I thought you could just waltz in and jack yourself up.

But since she was willing to deal with it, I agreed. *No biggie*, I thought to myself. I'd have this shopping-for-a-wedding-dress experience and then file it away along with other things I'd tried just so I could say I had done them, like the time I had sex with someone who owned a motorcycle (he told me only afterward that he had borrowed it from a friend aghhhhh…). Then I'd go spend a few hundred bucks on something at Bloomingdale's.

In the spirit of going full-tilt on the girliness of this excursion, I rounded up an extra friend and the three of us met at Cafe Cluny for a pre-shop champagne toast. I chugged it, got slightly more buzzed than I'd planned, and we crossed the street and entered Lovely.

Lovely is a quaint bridal boutique in the West Village, located on two floors of an old brownstone. Everyone on the sales staff is adorable and has impeccable yet approachable style. They all look like your big sister's best friend from Marin County. It is a place that has a reputation for attracting a more "low-key" (mid-thirties yuppie lady) bride and offering a more "curated" (less stuff) selection of dresses than big bridal warehouses like Kleinfeld. It's chockablock with the kinds of twee touches that make it catnip for girls: gilded antique mirrors, shabby chic chandeliers, and glass doorknobs. Little silver trays are filled with sparkling accessories: bracelets, rhinestone hairpins, and even—sadly—a tiara. A TIARA. But I'm not immune to catnip. I walked in and wanted a taste. I wanted to belong.

However, moments after we arrived, things started to go south. While we waited for the saleswoman who'd be helping us, I thought I'd get started and check out what was on the racks. No sooner had I taken a step away from the waiting area than one of the impeccable yet approachable women reprimanded me that I should not look at any dresses until I was accompanied by my attendant. "You can, like, look at the jewelry and hairpins that are where you're sitting," she said, in a tone that made it clear she was friendly, but not fucking around. This would be the deal at pretty much every bridal shop

I visited. For some reason that I never figured out, they do *not* like you to look at the stuff you will be looking at. Dresses are brought out from back rooms with somber reverence, like the Torah being revealed from the ark. Also, every appointment is exactly an hour, and then Cinderella time is over and it's time to get back to your stupid pumpkin life.

My saleswoman was "Maya," a pretty redhead with Amy Winehouse eyeliner. She was nice enough, but it was already four in the afternoon and she also seemed vaguely over it. Which made me insecure. Which was probably why she was over it. Who wants to deal with a bunch of insecure and needy girls all day? Maya followed me around the forbidden racks as I touched dress after dress, each of them covered in plastic, and tried to imagine myself as a bride. But for someone who normally wears jeans and an old sweater I'm trying to pretend I didn't buy at J.Crew in 2005, it was a tough road.

And it only got worse from there. I have a tremendous amount of inherent body shame but Maya made it clear, as she stepped behind the dressing room curtain with me, that she would not be granting me any privacy. As I fumbled around in front of this stranger in my raggy old Gap underwear and ill-fitting high heels, I waved good-bye to my dignity.

And I hadn't been familiar with the system for trying on the dresses, with the samples being either three sizes too big or (horror of horrors) four sizes too small. The ones that were too small I'd try to shimmy past my hips, then realize I had to give up. Under Maya's dead-eyed gaze I'd feel the pressure to make a self-deprecating joke, which would somehow make her eyes even deader.

The dresses that were too large, Maya would fasten to me with four or five construction-grade metal clips, so that I kind of looked like the old Victorian paper dolls I used to fasten paper dresses on top of until I got bored and waited for video games to be invented.

When we were able to get a dress vaguely on me, or even adjacent to me, I would shuffle out toward my friends and present myself on a little pedestal. From there we would engage in a verbal tennis match, wherein they would tell me I looked like the most beautiful angel ever to alight upon this earth, and I would tell them that I looked like a fat piece of shit, and they would tell me I was being insane, and then I would tell them they had to admit that my boobs were falling out of this dress that was clearly meant for a waifish mouse, and they would begrudgingly tell me that maybe perhaps the dress wasn't as gorgeous and special as I am, and then we'd settle there and I'd shuffle back into my dress cave.

Toward the end of my hour with Maya, who I could tell was really starting to fantasize about getting drunk at home by herself, I picked up one last dress that, once on, felt different. It was a strapless art deco column with sequins all over, and a blouson top.[1] I shuffled toward my friends and looked in the mirror. It was a beautiful

---

1   I don't know what *blouson* means.

dress—a wedding dress, yes, but with a boho-rock-star edge, a dress I could picture Kate Moss doing coke in before passing out on a huge messy bed at the Ritz. I took a moment to consider whether I wanted to look like a coked-up Kate Moss at my wedding, and realized the answer was yes. My friends told me I looked like the prettiest bride in the history of female creation. I thought my ass looked like a beanbag chair.

But now I'd seen myself in a wedding dress, and for the first time, saw a sliver of my potential to look like something besides myself for a day. Not even a day, I reasoned. Really, just a few hours. Maybe I could wear a wedding dress. Shouldn't I try to be feminine for just a few hours out of my entire fucking life?

And so the search began. I started looking online at wedding blogs, making lists. It was March. My wedding was in November. This seemed like a ton of time, although as Maya had warned me, before she went home to get stoned in the bathtub, for a November wedding I'd really want to order a dress by May. June at the latest. This seemed like an excessive amount of time for what I wanted, especially considering that I was going to get a very modest dress, nothing fancy, nothing expensive, most likely off the rack, basically rags.

In April, I had to go to LA for work, so I took the opportunity to meet with my friend Jenny (another person who was excited to take me wedding dress shopping) and go to Barneys. I tried on every iteration of white, champagne, and ivory party dress and I managed to look like a plump flamingo in all of them. I started to see a pattern, which is that my large boobs and hips, in combination with my stick arms and legs, made a lot of things that fit in one place not fit in another. Dresses that I thought looked good on me in the mirror would reveal themselves to be horribly unflattering when seen in the cold hard light of the photos Jenny was taking on her iPhone.

When Jenny had to leave for work, I Ubered my way over to the LA outpost of Lovely to see if they had "curated" any stock that wasn't in the New York store. This time the saleschick was a little bit sweeter, and, body shame a distant memory, we had a relatively pleasant time clipping me into a series of dresses that, like last time, all made me look like a large raccoon that had tipped over a garbage can searching for food, found a wedding dress instead, and then decided to take a nap in it.

Before leaving, I decided to take one final spin around to see if there was anything I'd missed, and in the corner rack I noticed a strapless dress with a multi-tiered bottom. It looked odd on the rack, falling in a weird shape from the hanger. It was the Charlie Brown Christmas tree of dresses. But once it was on, I felt something, a lightness. It had a bohemian whimsy. It looked like a cross between the costume of a bawdy nineteenth-century saloon owner and something Frida Kahlo would have worn to paint herself bleeding to death. I looked like a bride who didn't take being a bride too seriously, not like one of those women on the cover of *Brides* magazine who looks like her facial expression is being held in place with toothpicks.

The saleschick jacked me up with a sparkly sash, and looking in the mirror, I felt good. I looked like me, but more female-er. I immediately sent photos to four or five friends to get their blessings so I could end this ridiculous process.

One friend texted "pretty," but then there was a pause, and then those three little iPhone dots that mean someone is writing you back appeared again, and this continued for a while before the message was finally SENT and she said, "I've never really liked ruffles?..."

All the texts I got back were decidedly tepid. No one else LOVED it.

A seed of doubt was planted, but I still felt pretty confident I'd found my dress. Maybe I'd just go to a few places to see if I could find something better. But in a week or two, if I couldn't, I'd just buy it. After all, who gives a shit? I made an appointment at Saks in New York.

Saks New York's bridal salon had glass doors separating the bridal parlor from the rest of the upscale shopper riffraff. My saleswoman, Barbara, was an older lady from New Jersey who told me she'd been at this for twenty-five years. She was a familiar type to me, maternal ambiguous Jew-Italian, and she seemed kind. I trusted her. Ten minutes into the appointment she came back into my dressing room dragging behind her several large plastic garment bags, which looked as heavy as if they contained corpses, but were filled instead with glittering sheaths.

They were all beautiful, but there was one small problem. Just a month earlier, Baz Luhrmann's *The Great Gatsby*
had premiered and every fashion magazine was filled with
Gatsby-inspired dresses, all of which looked like these, and
I felt like some Zelda Fitzgerald–wannabe asshole.

The one nice thing was how encouraging Barbara was
about my body. "You don't have anything to worry about,
you're like a model, you'll look good in anything," she
said. But midway through my hour, I started telling her
about the tiered dress from Lovely and how I was looking
for something with that same whimsical vibe. "Show me,"
she said. I showed her the photo on my phone and she
scowled. "No," she said, her voice dripping with disgust.
"It's like a maternity dress. You look pregnant."

My heart sank. Even Barbara had turned on me.

This was the first moment I started to realize that some
larger problem was boiling to the surface, that this wasn't
just about the dress, but rather a deep cauldron of self-
doubt in my own taste—and not just my own taste, but
my entire self. It was one thing to be a sartorial mess in
my everyday life, but it felt like quite another to show
up at my own wedding in something that everyone would
silently think was an embarrassment. I'd spent my whole
life walking around with a certain relief that when I entered a room I wasn't one of those girls everyone stared
at. But in this case, as the bride, by definition I was the
one everyone was supposed to gawk at. This was terrifying. To fail at finding a wedding dress felt like failing
at femininity. What if I COULDN'T pull it together for

a few measly hours? What would that say about me as a woman? And how disappointing would it be for Mike, who looks impeccable every day?

A quick word on Mike—about two months into my dress search, he decided it was time to find a suit. I went with him on a Saturday afternoon to Prada. I was prepared to comfort him, to tell him not to be discouraged when nothing fit. Within twenty minutes, he found a suit that looked perfect on him the moment he tried it on. He bought it, and we went home.

Total wedding suit search time: an hour and forty-five minutes. I wanted to murder him. I wanted to murder everyone.

I was becoming unglued. Finding a dress became a job, with whole days spent running from one place to another, heels and a strapless bra always in my bag, like I was a hybrid of superhero and stripper. I made an appointment at Nicole Miller, where I found a dress that I loved except for the fact that my boobs were spilling out of the cups. Me and the salesgirl, who was busy planning her own wedding, had an increasingly contentious conversation about whether the dress could be altered for my body. She insisted it could work, and stuck about thirty pins into the top to create a simulation of how the dress, once tailored, could offer more coverage, but the effect was like trying to cover a wombat with a cocktail napkin.

I also struck out at a newly opened "bohemian" studio where the owner sat in front of her MacBook Air twisting flowers into headwreaths while I tried on vintage hippie dresses inside a tinsel-strewn yurt. I'd held out big hopes for this place, but everything I tried on made me look like someone half-assing a Stevie Nicks Halloween costume, and at the end of my appointment my friend Kate and I fled to go get drunk.

I eventually broke down and went to Kleinfeld, where I'd hear spontaneous bursts of applause as bride after bride said yes after yes to dress after dress.

All this time, I thought about the tiered dress like an old lover I couldn't get out of my head, occasionally casting wistful looks at the pictures of it on my phone. On Memorial Day, my friend Eleanor came over and we locked ourselves in my bedroom as Mike made cheeseburgers in the kitchen.

"I think I have to buy the tiered dress, I can't handle this shit anymore," I whined. I begged her to give me permission to just buy it.

"You look beautiful in the dress," she said, looking at the photo.

"You sure?" I asked her.

"Yes," she said.

I picked up my laptop to order the dress online, but right before I hit SUBMIT PAYMENT she blurted out: "I'm worried about the first tier, I think it hits you at an awkward spot." I looked at her. There was desperation in her eyes, and I knew she felt awful. It was as if she'd unburdened herself of a terrible secret that could destroy both of our lives. We've known each other since we were eleven years old, when she wore Mickey Mouse suspenders and I wore a nightbrace. I knew she loved me. She wouldn't say something if it wasn't true.

This is how I found myself the next morning, in ninety-five-degree heat, sweating my way to Bergdorf Goodman, a department store that I'd never set foot in, despite having lived in New York almost my entire life. I'd imagined it was too posh for me. I was right.

I skulked the halls like Javier Bardem's terrifying villain in *No Country for Old Men*, a broken husk, running my hands lightly along sequined gowns and then moving on, hunting down my target.

And then I saw it. A bright-white beaded A-line cocktail dress; not a wedding dress, but better, timeless. Valentino. I picked up my pace, practically jogging toward it. Up close, it shimmered magically. I grabbed it in my size and ran into the dressing room.

I looked in the mirror, and for the first time since I'd started this whole ridiculous chase, I felt that I knew with certainty, the way Oprah knows certain things FOR SURE, that this was my wedding dress. I snapped nervous selfies in the mirror, and even with my sweaty chest and flushed face, I thought I looked just a bit like Audrey Hepburn. I looked like Audrey Hepburn if Audrey Hepburn was Jewish and had narrowly escaped a burning building. Nevertheless, I felt I could work with this look. The sense of relief that I'd found the dress of my dreams, and not just my dreams, but probably everyone's dreams, was so intense that I hadn't even bothered looking at the price tag, but it was scratching me somewhere around my neck so I twisted to see it.

Nine thousand nine hundred and ninety-nine dollars.

$$$$$!!!!☹

I began to ponder the difference—financially, spiritually—between something that costs ten thousand dollars and something that is one hundred pennies less. My budget, which at the beginning of this process had been a hard-and-fast two grand, had been rising at an alarming rate. At Kleinfeld, I'd tried on something very pretty that was over five thousand dollars and had decided that five thousand bucks was the absolute bar-is-closing, get-a-fucking-life limit. And here I was, in something more than twice that price, hearing some weird voice telling me to just go for it. I looked around. There was no one else in the dressing room. Holy shit, the voice was coming from inside my own head.

I began a long, spiraling, nonsensical internal monologue justifying the purchase of the dress. "Here's what I'm gonna do," I whispered to myself. "I'll put this dress on my credit card, and I will simply never tell anyone about how much I spent, not ever. I will lie to anyone who asks, including Mike, about where I bought this, what it cost, and even who makes it. No one needs to know it's Valentino. I can say I bought it at Loehmann's. When my credit card statement comes, I will give it a Viking funeral on the East River. Furthermore, I was poor as a child, and if I add it up, ten thousand dollars probably just about covers what I'm owed from my poor childhood. No one will ever ever know, and since this isn't technically a wedding dress, I can wear it again to, like, a garden party, or someone else's wedding, or even the gym. I'm owed this dress. It would be wrong not to get it. I want it and it's okay and I was poor and I'm gonna lie and it's fine."

At this point in the monologue, I had the sudden realization that the completely illogical circular argument I was building was not unlike what men must tell themselves as they plan to murder their wives.

I stared at myself in the mirror, and then slowly took off the dress and put it back on the hanger. I packed up my strapless bra and my heels and walked to the 6 train and went home. I called my friend Becky and cried about how I'd lost my bearings, how the idea of choosing the wrong dress had become paralyzing, but mostly, I lamented that I had become someone I didn't recognize, the worst kind of cliché. Becky, bless her, talked me off the ledge. She reassured me that every bride goes through this, and I was putting too much pressure on myself, and generally kept talking in a calm voice until I started breathing again. Somehow her words sank in, and when Becky hung up, I called Lovely, ordered the stupid tiered dress, and then had a ~~bottle~~ glass of wine to celebrate the hundred-pound weight I had just thrown off myself, like Chief tossing the sink through the window at the end of *One Flew Over the Cuckoo's Nest.* Yes, IT WAS JUST LIKE THAT.

We think of the bridezilla as this insatiable, bitchy dragon, breathing fire through a constantly inflamed temper, devouring the patience of anyone who dares to defy her whims. I was a bridezilla, but in reverse. Feeling the heat of impossible expectations, I spent months throwing daggers at my own reflection.

Toward the end of my wedding, drunk and joyful, I grabbed a girlfriend to help me pull the dress off and slip into a cheapish little shift I'd brought along just in case I wanted to change. I threw the wedding dress onto a heap of coats without a second thought.

When Mike and I got back to our hotel suite at the end of the night, I discovered that the wedding planner had already brought it back, carefully zipped into its garment bag. That bag is now at the back of my closet. I've only peeked inside once. The dress's hem is blackish with soot, and there are wine stains all over the front. Mike says I should clean it, but I'm not going to bother.

Long Day's Journey into Porn

They say that women don't like porn. I used to think I didn't like porn, but now here I am on my bed, on my stomach, just moments after Mike has left for work, typing four x's into my Google search window. They will lead me to a porn site where I will scroll through a series of thumbnails offering a panoply of sexual images, from the banal to the genuinely horrifying, until I find something I think I can work with. Minutes later, I am done, experiencing that feeling every guy friend I've ever discussed this topic with has described, of going from highly revved up to vaguely repulsed with myself, and then stuffing the whole experience into a mental dirty laundry hamper and moving on with my day.

I have become someone who masturbates to porn. That is actually only part of the truth, and to be honest it's the part that I have no problem admitting. After all, we now live in a pornified world where it almost feels like a greater effort not to look at porn than to be staring at it constantly. What bothers me is not that I now have a porn habit, but rather that after almost three decades of old-fashioned, pornless diddling, I've lost almost all interest in masturbating without it.

Which means that looking at porn has somehow rewired a primitive, reptilian neural pathway in my brain in such a way that I am now jerking off like a man.

How did this happen?

A brief history of my experience with porn:

I was born in 1975. I came of age in those long-lost sepia years when porn was something that had to be meticulously searched for and excavated. Magazines and videos were surreptitiously stashed in hiding places by fathers and brothers, like so many filthy afikomen. The purchasing of such materials usually required you to man (or woman) up and acknowledge, to at least one other live human being standing in front of you, the specific shameful needs of your erotic life.

In fact, from a relatively young age, I was very interested in naked people and nudity. Because there was no Internet, and we didn't have cable (my parents didn't even give up their rotary phone until well into the 1990s), the bar for what was sexually exciting to me was extremely low. Around the age of nine or ten, after discovering a pair of binoculars somewhere in our apartment, I developed a serious peeping tom habit. At night I would stand behind the curtains at one of our windows and scan the lit windows of the building complex across the street, waiting for some unsuspecting citizen to walk through his or her apartment in a towel on the way to or from the shower. The shades were often half down, which meant I would only catch a glimpse of a pair of pasty legs. And it was a building whose demographic was primarily over fifty, so the flesh I saw was often a little loose. No matter. Just the fact of seeing what was not meant to be seen would give me a little shiver.

In third grade, even though I was extremely shy and didn't really have friends, I enjoyed a brief surge in popularity when I attracted attention for my ability to draw naked people. I was a gifted artist (according to my parents) who had been drawing horses and dogs to great acclaim (from my parents) for many years, but one day I suddenly found myself inspired to tackle this new subject matter. My seatmates noticed me drawing these anatomically correct(ish) figures and were fascinated. I can't remember if I drew them in sexual positions or not; I think maybe sometimes I just drew them kissing, or even lying on top of each other, like planks but otherwise emotionless. Pretty soon during free period I was surrounded by a cluster of my peers as I dashed off naked people, like a nine-year-old-girl version of Picasso handing out scribbles as payment for meals. This went on until my teacher noticed what was happening and immediately alerted our principal, most likely out of concern that I was being molested (fair enough).

Our principal was a brilliant and gentle man from New Zealand named John Meltzer, a freethinker who rightly became a legend after his death and for whom the school is now named. John called me into his office for a meeting.

I was a very good kid who never got into trouble, so I was extremely nervous. He sat me down across from him and, with a bemused look on his face, asked me:

"Jessi, love. Why are you drawing naked people?"

"Um…I don't know."

After a few more questions, John seemed satisfied I wasn't a victim of a crime, but rather just a young pervert in the making; to interfere would prevent me from becoming my most authentic self. It was a Montessori school, after all.

I was released back into the wild.

In fifth grade I became friends with a girl named Margo who had a classically shady stepfather: long-haired, unemployed, and possessing a slurred manner of speaking that made it impossible to understand a word he said, which was probably for the best. One afternoon Margo and I went to the movies. Afterward, we were sitting in the theater lobby finishing a box of Junior Mints when she asked if I wanted to do something "fun." She told me that her stepfather and his friends had been hanging out in the house calling phone sex lines on speakerphone and laughing their asses off (because what else would you do for fun with your friends when you live with a ten-year-old girl?). I was not familiar with phone sex lines but I was intrigued. We found a pay phone in the corner of the lobby and came up with the sixty quarters needed to dial a phone sex line from a pay phone. We then both put our ears to the receiver and listened to a recording of a lady saying something, if I remember correctly, about how horny she was getting while inserting a tooth-brush in her vagina. Most likely I am not remembering this correctly, seeing as how that makes no sense, but I do distinctly recall the orgasmic moans and groans this dis-embodied voice was making and how darkly exciting they were, even more stimulating than old-people legs seen from three hundred feet away.

Over the next few weeks, anytime I was home alone I would call this sex line and listen to these moany record-ings, trying to understand what they were making me feel. I probably called about twenty-five times. I was oblivious to the fact that they cost money until about a month later when my mother approached me with a funny look on her face and asked if I had made any un-usual phone calls. My blood froze as, without thinking twice, I straight-up lied and said no. My mother moved on, surely confirming in her mind that it made much more sense that the culprit must be my fourteen-year-old brother.

After that I was spooked. I didn't know where to look for porn, but even if I had, the risk of being caught seemed too high. Besides, about two years later, while I was lying on my stomach in my room, doing social stud-ies homework and listening to horribly cheesy pop radio, some terrible techno song came on that featured a part in the middle during which the beat slowed down to ac-commodate the sounds of a woman having a prolonged orgasm. I do not know how this was cleared for FM air-play, but I felt a funny Judy Blume–ish feeling near my pubic bone, and sixty seconds later I had learned how to masturbate.

But I didn't need porn. In addition to my cheesy techno song, I was also titillated when people on soap operas kissed. And I'm talking about afternoon prime-time soap operas in the '80s, not anything even basic cable edgy. Just two white people in crewneck sweaters kissing for three seconds before a tasteful fade to commercial was all it took to fuel my most torrid fantasies.

The one other visual stimulus I remember obsessing over was the video for Billy Idol's "Cradle of Love," which featured a blond girl in booty shorts named "Devon" doing splits on a bed while a nerdy white guy hid in the corner of his apartment, terrified of this sexy girl and her subversive Billy Idol tape. This video was my equivalent of hard-core filth although in reality it was just dancing and light pillow fighting.

What all of these naughty little blips had in common, aside from their G-ratedness, was that in the pre-Internet age, they could not be voluntarily summoned. I had to patiently wait for them to appear, like a bird-watcher waiting to see a sexy canary. But it was enough for me, and I never once thought about going through the process of trying to procure anything genuinely graphic, partially because I didn't care and partially because it seemed like too much work. This was confirmed for me when, during my summers home from college in New York, I worked as a clerk at a delightful neighborhood video store in Chelsea run by a very nice man named Adam.

Adam was a fatherly type who prided himself on running a "family-friendly" shop, but he was also a businessman, which meant that the store still had a small porn section in the back. To remain "family-friendly," Adam instituted an arduous procedure through which customers could rent their porn without disturbing the *Jumanji* crowd. In the filth corner in the back, there was a pile of scraps of paper and little golf pencils. Customers wanting to rent porn would write their titles of interest on the scraps of paper, and then come up to the counter and wordlessly hand them to me, the nineteen-year-old girl who was tasked with fetching their VHS cassettes. I would silently go check on whether *Buttman's Bubble Butt Babes* (a very popular title at the time) or *Cinesex* (slightly less popular) was available, which it often wasn't. I would then go back to the customer at the counter and say, "We don't have this one or this one," handing them back their slips of paper, at which point they would retreat back to the porn room and start over. It broke my heart when this process had to be repeated several times over, knowing that these customers were going to be masturbating to their fifth or sixth choice of tapes.

My lack of curiosity around porn was also a result of the fact that my boyfriend Pete didn't seem interested in porn. I never once found anything incriminating around the house or on his computer. True, it was still the early days of the Internet, and his laptop was one of those tangerine clamshell Macs that seemed to have been beamed upon us from a futuristic Martian society when in fact they had the Internet speed of bird feeders.

In retrospect, the best evidence for Pete's lack of interest in porn was our sex life, which could be generously described as perfectly average. It wasn't until years later, after we broke up and I started dating for basically the first time in my life, that I saw how things could be different.

My second boyfriend after Pete was Harrison, moodily handsome, darkly funny, and sexy in a way that was foreign to me. He had a shaved head and biceps that he had actually put real effort into. He was more soccer hooligan than nerd hipster. He told me stories about walking down a nude beach when he was visiting Australia and having a chat with a beautiful topless Australian girl who became his girlfriend. He drank a lot and had a chin-up bar in his bedroom doorway. And yet, he was deeply sensitive, even depressed; and for these reasons, I fell in love with him.

Because I'd only had sex with one person for a long time, I was prepared for it to be a different experience. What I was not prepared for was sex in the age of Internet porn, and how interested Harrison was in ejaculating on my body, and then, gradually, when I didn't flee or register protest over that act, my face. I was unhappily surprised by it, but I was so timid about my lack of experience at the advanced age of twenty-seven that I didn't want to ask any of my plentiful follow-up questions, among which were:

1. Why did you want to come on my face?
2. How do you think I feel about you coming on my face?
3. Is this A Thing everyone is doing?
4. What gave you the idea to do this?[1]

The answer to #4, of course, was Internet porn. I didn't know this yet. I was at the very beginning of this new trend where masses of young men learn how to have sex from watching porn. But I didn't make this connection, not even when I innocently went on his desktop computer one afternoon to check my email and, upon pressing a random key, threw off the cover of his "sleep" screen to reveal the activity underneath, which was a browser frozen on hundreds of thumbnails of the most filthy German porn, creating a mosaic of naked genitals and random objects being recruited into unimaginable penetrations.

At first I was embarrassed for him; and then, when I realized I could neither unfreeze the computer nor put it back into sleep mode, I was way more embarrassed for me. There was nothing to do when he came back from the bathroom but to explain that I had not meant to snoop, and yet here I was staring at fifty gaping buttholes. I wasn't mad, which was good, seeing as he wasn't anything more than slightly sheepish. He was primarily ashamed of

---

1   The answers, in order—1. Porn. 2. Don't care. 3. Yes because of porn. 4. Porn.

the fact that his masturbation habits had brought a rather expensive Dell desktop to its knees. He ended up needing to buy a new computer.

The one thing to which he did confess was that he'd been watching maybe a bit too much porn in the last year, and now he felt he needed to stop.

"I think it's affecting the way I have sex" was what he said.

I wanted to say, "Yeah, it's funny, I was thinking the same thing right when you ejaculated into my eye the other night," but I felt that might be impolite.

I didn't want to be the kind of person who looked down on anyone for using porn, and intellectually, I wasn't. And yet—I was distrustful of it. I can't emphasize enough how badly semen stings in your eye. It's worse than shampoo. If there was a Johnson & Johnson's "No more tears" version of semen, I might have felt differently. But the whole episode put a strain on my and porn's already thin relationship.

Which brings us to my current situation.

A few years ago, I was dating a man I liked very much. I was always worried about whether he felt the same way, and as a result, I was often jealous. I wish I could say I went on his computer to check my email but that would be a big fat lie because the truth is I wanted to dig through his Internet history. I had to click past oodles of ESPN.com and sneaker site visits, but with enough scrolling I eventually dug up what I was looking for, which is to say, anything that would annoy me and make me feel terrible about myself. A pile of sites with x's followed by backslashes followed by various adjectives of different female body types rose from the bottom of the screen. And maybe because I was so jealous, and was so worried about being what he wanted, I felt compelled to look at what he was looking at, to see if it in any way matched up with what I am. (Because obviously that is why men turn to porn. To find women who look like the women they're with.) Like an idiot, I was holding out hope of finding a site filled with videos of pale, bespectacled Jewish girls with their hair up in sloppy buns.

Spoiler alert: That's not what he was looking at.

The truth is, what he was looking at wasn't that bad. I was actually relieved to see that it was all middle-of-the-road sex stuff (relatively speaking). For the sake of this story, what matters is that for the first time in my life, I found myself looking at a porn site and feeling—could it be?—genuine curiosity.

I didn't know anything about Internet porn, and it took me a while to find my way, like having to learn the geography of the new mall in your town. It takes a while to know where the good stuff is. (Where's the J.Crew? The Sephora?) The site I'd found was an aggregator, with hundreds of videos to look at, organized into a long list of alphabetical categories on the left side of the screen. These categories range from basics like "amateur" to something called "real amateur" (which makes me wonder what all those people going to the fake amateur category are thinking); there are job categories, like "doctor" and "nurse," if you are turned on by watching someone who makes a good income and can find work anywhere have sex; there are classic hard-core things like "anal" and "deep throat"; and then there are links for weirder, more specific fetishes like "pregnant," which I have never clicked on, but even just knowing it exists makes me feel a sad lonely feeling in the deepest part of my heart. It might be because as I am writing this chapter I am pregnant (surprise!)[2] and I am annoyed at tying my shoes, so I can't even fathom having to pretend I am LOVING some rando's dick.

But I wasn't pregnant when I started looking at this site, and even then, the gestalt of the thing overwhelmed me. If you try to click on one of the tamer categories, like "massage" (which usually starts with light foot rubs but often ends in sexual gore), and you forget to enlarge your video to full screen, you are forced to simultaneously watch GIF banner ads all over the rest of the window, which always feature comically grotesque imagery of ladies definitely, how shall I say, not being made love to.

There are so many things on there I don't want to see (all of which I've now seen):

1. Women sobbing while having sex.
2. Women being choked while having sex.

---

2   That's how long it takes to write a book. The writing of this book has spanned being barren, then conceiving, and then growing a human. The majority of this book was written by a not-pregnant person.

3. Anyone sobbing or being choked while having sex.
4. A live-action person having sex with an animated alien.
5. A female little person being doggy-styled by a normal-size person.

But still. I'm still human. The part of me that stood behind curtains as a tweenager with an old pair of binoculars, hoping against hope to see someone's knees peeking out from under a towel, still was excited to see naked people. Except I didn't want to see the Hieronymus Bosch version of sex. Ironically, after decades of porn being something you had to pry out of secret drawers and basements and forests, I now had to dig through an endlessly available, 24/7 porn delivery service to excavate videos of people, who seem to at least be on an amicable acquaintance basis, having regular, plain old sex.[3]

The first time I employed porn for an assist in pleasuring myself, I felt tremendous guilt. Not because I'd "sinned" looking at porn, but more because I felt guilty that I was no longer a member of the analog masturbation world. I'd gone digital. It was similar to the feeling I had when I gave up my old-school flip Samsung cell and bought an iPhone. Now I was like everyone else, kind of. Why couldn't I just use my imagination anymore? What

---

3   Don't get me wrong—I want the people to be better looking than me. But I want them to look like mammals who breathe air and bear their young, not implanted reptiles or furious velociraptors.

was happening to me? Why didn't I still have a record player? And besides, wasn't I a girl? Wasn't I not supposed to like any porn at all?

But I do. I like the kind of porn that I like. It's so much more than what I needed to titillate me as a kid, but now, apparently, compared with everyone else in the world, much less. I do not know how many other women look at porn, or under what circumstances. I know that as of this writing, as I am seven months pregnant, it has been incredibly helpful, since my panda-like stomach has made sex with my husband difficult to impossible. Even watching the very simple porn that I scrabble around to find is an air supply to an erotic life I often worry will evaporate as I become a mother, a sweet Proustian madeleine to remembering what it was like to be an object of new desire; to have a body that belonged only to me and whoever I deigned to share it with. I know those days are numbered.

The other night Mike was out of town and I was enjoying a quiet hour in bed before going to sleep. I was working on my baby registry, adding the last few items my son will need, among which is (apparently?) a humidifier. With my laptop leaning against my knees and belly, I went on Amazon and scrolled through a surprisingly long list of options. Some had animal-like features (there was one that was shaped like an elephant with an elephant trunk that spewed mist), and others were more clinical. Which would he like better? I started reading user reviews, comments from other parents about which ones are easy to clean, which make the room too humid…which…which…which…and I got bored.

It had been a while.

I opened another tab, and typed in the x's. I found a video. A man is kissing a woman's neck, and then he takes off her bra. They seem to like each other well enough. No one sobs or chokes.

They finish. I finish. I close out of the window with the x's and by default I am back on my last webpage, face-to-face with the elephant humidifier. At first it feels like the proximity of these two tabs is a bit profane—these things shouldn't have been so close to each other. But then I think, *Well, isn't all this part of life.* Birth and sex and porn. Exciting and horrible and great and disgusting and joyful.

Leap of Faith

In 2007, Oprah Winfrey and her best friend Gayle went to Miraval Spa, a wellness facility in Tucson, Arizona, to do what was then known as the "Leap of Faith." The "Leap of Faith" involves climbing to the top of a twenty-five-foot wooden pole, somehow transitioning from the pole to the shaky disk perched at its top, declaring an intention about what in your life you want to leave behind, and then jumping off, at which point you are gently belayed down by a facilitator as well as your new friends, the six other women in your group who are also doing the Leap of Faith.

At the time, my friend Becky and I were both around thirty and serious Oprah obsessives. We watched the episode intently from our separate homes, and then got on the phone to discuss. Oprah, who even back then had already had about a billion "aha" moments, was having her mind blown at the top of this tricked-out telephone pole. The Leap of Faith had burned into our souls. We spoke of one day making the pilgrimage to this sacred place and performing this magical act.

Eight years later, I am taking a Delta flight from NYC to Tucson (with one stop in Atlanta). Becky is flying from Philadelphia and we will meet there. In the time that has passed between watching Oprah on TV and packing our bags, Becky and I have been through many boyfriends and many more breakups, one of which is fresh for Becky. She is also turning forty. I am engaged and getting married in three months, a source of joy but also extreme terror. With everything that's happened to us, we now have a clearer understanding of what Miraval is. Which is to say, it's a place for women like us. A place where women who are scared, angry, or going through a divorce or some other painful life transition flock to figure their shit out. Although it's coed, very, very few men go there, because men don't feel the need to leap off a pole to understand their lives.

A few days before leaving, Becky and I compared notes on the activities that we (and her mom, who is tagging along) would be booking during our stay. Miraval's website offers a truly staggering number of things you can have someone do to you. Guided Photography Walks, Tibetan Chakra Cleansing, Aerial Yoga classes, acupuncture, and "Soul Journeys," just to name a few. If a Soul Journey sounds too overwhelming, you can also take a more modest "Pedicure Journey." To help you assess what might interest you, the site offers a questionnaire, which will determine your "color" and "shape," signifiers in their symbolic emotional grid. After answering a series of questions about whether I am bold and adventurous or anxious and shitty, I discovered I am an "Orange Diamond," meaning I am an optimistic explorer. This was a shock, because when I filled out the questionnaire I tried very hard to accurately communicate my anxious shittiness. I'd been certain I'd end up a Blue Circle or perhaps a Mauve Star of David. The Miraval algorithm produced about fifteen suggested activities appropriate for an Orange Diamond, including a private lesson called "Riding the Wave."

Becky and I were both particularly intrigued by a woman on the site named "Tejpal." One name, like Madonna or Cher. She was billed as a Brennan Healing Practitioner, which meant nothing to me even after I looked it up, but mainly I was fascinated by her photo. She looked like a sort of beautiful 1970s woodland creature, with a wily short gray haircut, tan skin, angled features, and a big smile. She looked like a line drawing from the original edition of *The Joy of Sex*, and had the sinewy build of someone subsisting solely on carob.

With my insanely generous number of "girls' getaway package" resort credits, I booked a different kind of massage for every day I was there: an ayurvedic massage, a Swedish massage, and something called "Tranquil Nights," which promised that the conclusion of the treatment would involve me getting "rocked to sleep." I wondered whether this was a euphemism for a happy ending and decided I was fine with being surprised.

Becky arrived at Miraval two days before I did, and I think she'd maybe been there two hours when she texted me, "Word on the street is Tejpal's amazing."

DAY ONE

On my flight to Tucson, I sat next to a well-attired woman in her mid-sixties who had a beautiful Louis Vuitton suitcase tucked under the seat in front of her. Though she read throughout most of the trip, she tapped me about thirty minutes before we landed. "You might want to take a peek at some of this scenery." I looked out the window at the majestic rust-colored mountains, and we started chatting. She'd lived outside Tucson for fifty years, although her job as a Bible textbook writer took her around the world.

As she politely pointed out the landmarks we were passing over, I couldn't help but think, *Even though we are totally from different worlds, most people are basically decent. We can all get along.* I was feeling proud of the connections I was already making on my trip to the Southwest when she tapped me again.

"Now you can see we're entering ranch territory. Arizona has a lot of cattle."

"Oh right, yes I've heard that," I said.[1]

She continued, "The only problem is that the Mexicans often come around and kill 'em. That's why we *have* to build that fence."

---

1 I hadn't.

"So what kind of house do you live in?" I inquired, as I began the more familiar process of disliking this hateful stranger.

I arrived at Miraval in the early afternoon, where Becky was eagerly waiting for me in the lobby. "Tejpal is talking in forty-five minutes." I raced to put my bag down in my room, where there was a series of stacked shelves labeled COURAGE, CONFIDENCE, CLARITY, BALANCE.

Although the grounds of Miraval were stunning, the meeting rooms were smaller and more corporate looking than I had expected. One thing I noticed immediately, as we walked down the hall on our way to Tejpal Ground Zero, was the presence of tissue boxes. Tissue boxes were in every room, perched quietly on every extra surface. One room we passed had a circle of seven chairs, and within that circle, on the floor, a circle of seven Kleenex boxes. I shuddered at the idea of a gathering where the certainty of every attendee having a nervous breakdown was so concrete.

We walked into the Tejpal conference room, where a group of about fifteen women was assembling. The demographic in this room would be representative of the people I met over the next few days: women ranging from their late thirties to early fifties, usually still in the Lululemon pants and tops they had worn to hike or lounge about the property. These women were mostly tan and, although of varying weight, all physically fit. Everyone kind of looked like Elizabeth Gilbert. Kind-faced, interesting, and interested.

But the last woman who walked in the room was different from the rest. Although I guessed she was in her midforties, she looked older, not younger, than her age. She had dyed-black hair, Dracula eyeliner, and an unhealthy pallor. Clothing-wise, she was more Real Housewife (of Long Island) than *SELF* magazine.

Tejpal began by telling us that the goal of being alive was to live with vitality. Projected on a screen was a PowerPoint presentation illustrating the onion-like layers of our being, going from "physical" at the outer layer to "spiritual" at the core. Though Tejpal looked just like her picture but with longer hair, I was shocked to discover that (1) she was French, and (2) her speaking voice was almost identical to Elmo's. She had a way of phrasing ideas where she would say something extremely profound, followed by a whimsically contradictory dismissal of what had just been said. So it was like, "The most eemportant theeng to remember about your life iz to fully commit to every theeng you do. But also, who can care about evereething, life iz crazy, who cares?"

What gets in the way of living with vitality? Tejpal asked.

Everything, I thought to myself.

Wounds, Tejpal said.

She talked about the importance of forgiveness, and how the most important step in forgiveness is to allow yourself to feel the pain of the hurt you received. Only then would the pain begin to heal.

Suddenly, Dracula leaned forward and spoke up, even

though this wasn't really a situation where you were supposed to speak without being called on. "That's not true," she blurted out angrily, her Long Island accent pulling all her vowels downward. "There are some things people do that hurt you forever. And they cause scars that will never heal. Just because you think about them doesn't mean they're goin' away." All the women in the room turned around to stare at this angry person. This was supposed to be a touchy-feely self-discovery happy place where Tejpal was in charge. You were not supposed to attack Tejpal.

I sensed that people thought she was crazy, and normally I would find her as annoying for not *getting it* as everyone else was, but instead I felt a wave of deep compassion. It was the first time during my visit to Miraval that I felt attuned to how deeply, painfully exposed people can allow themselves to be when there's even a sliver of permission to be honest.

Tejpal simply said, "That iz your beleef system, not mine."

I felt my heart breaking for Dracula.

That night, after dinner, I went for my Tranquil Nights Massage. I'd been up since five thirty a.m. and I was exhausted. A nice blond mouse of a woman led me to the outdoor hut where I'd receive the service. I remember choosing a scent (Relax by Clarins) and getting on the table, and I remember her switching off the overhead light for string lights, and I remember the whole place feeling like an enchanted Bedouin tent. But the moment she touched me I started to doze, and then I was dreaming soft wellness spa dreams. I had never fallen asleep during a massage before, because normally I cannot even fall asleep in my own bed without 5 mg of Ambien.[2] But here I was, snoozing away. I discovered that sleeping during a massage is a mixed experience, because on the one hand you are completely relaxed, but on the other hand you wake up to a total stranger kneading your glutes.

When it was over, I walked back to my adobe cottage, jelly-legged, and I was struck by two things. First, the temperature of the air. It felt like the exact temperature of my own body, so it was difficult to tell where my skin ended and the outside world began. The second thing was the stars. I looked up to see, for the first time in my life, the ghost-chalk whiteness between all the stars, the milk in the Milky Way. I was so happy I felt like crying. Not to worry—when I got back to my room, I found three strategically placed tissue boxes perched at different points around the bed, bathroom, and sitting area, waiting for me.

DAY TWO

The next morning, my schedule was packed. I had another massage (I know), a class called "Athletology," and a private session wherein I would learn how to "Ride the Wave."

I walked to the spa, slipped into a robe, and went to

---

2   Actually 10 mg.

the "quiet room" to wait. In the quiet room sat a copy of *Condé Nast Traveler* with a big article about Miraval, so you could read about Miraval while being at Miraval. But the article could not compete with the scenery. The room had a giant floor-to-ceiling window so you could look out at the mountains. The morning sun moved across them dramatically, painting one peak dark purple and then brilliant yellow. I stared at them, thinking about how breathtaking mountains are and how crazy it was that I, as a New York City kid, had never really seen them until now. Suddenly I heard a tapping sound and turned to see the woman in the chaise lounge next to me ignoring the mountains in favor of playing Candy Crush on her iPad, tapping away with a perfectly manicured nail.

I had my second stupidly wonderful massage and then rushed to Athletology, another class in another corporate-looking conference room. About twenty women piled in, once again tanned and Lululemoned, and once again the exception was sad Dracula, who had changed into some-what bedazzled gold-accented loungewear. Our leader this time was a woman going by the handle "Coach Leigh," and the minute she entered the room, I felt a strong urge to be her. She was about six feet tall and broad-shouldered, with long swinging brown hair and more than a passing resemblance to supermodel volleyball player Gabrielle Reece. Everything about her radiated confidence and optimism. She began by explaining that she'd been a tennis junior pro, and pointed out that all athletes listen to music to get psyched for the task at hand. "I don't want you to be any different," she said, and told us that she was going to play us a song in its entirety, during which we were to write the answer to the question "Who am I?" and I was open to this idea until she started to play "Man in the Mirror" by Michael Jackson, at which point I just started writing "what the fuck am I doing here" over and over again for three minutes.

But post-song, things improved as she explained that everything she ever learned during her life in sports felt 100 percent applicable to everyday life. The notion of optimism less as a choice but simply as a necessary part of winning, the idea of changing your life just 5 percent every day to get huge changes in what you can achieve, and more than anything, the idea that in order to play your best game you must let go of caring about the outcome of the game, and that herein was the secret to happiness. And about twelve minutes into her talk, as her good vibes shimmered across the room, I felt something I had never felt before: namely, how embarrassing it feels to be genuinely inspired by an inspirational speaker. Because in that moment, at the same time you're getting excited for the clarity with which you can suddenly see your life, creeping up right behind it is a rain cloud of shame that it's come to this.

After Athletology, feeling like a real Orange Diamond, I zipped over to the main lobby where I would meet Dr. Smith, the man who was going to teach me about "Riding the Wave." It would be a one-on-one session, meaning that I had paid over $200 for this conversation to be just between us. The saddest thing was that between signing up for this class and now getting ready to attend it I had lost all memory of what it was about or what had motivated me to choose it in the first place. This feeling only got worse when Dr. Smith emerged and called out my name, and I looked up to see a man dressed in billowy pin-striped pants, a short-sleeved collared shirt, and a vinyl visor, all of this centered on a face that looked exactly, and I mean exactly, like that of Jim Carrey in *Dumb and Dumber*.

If you're waiting for me to tell you how to "Ride the Wave," or even what that means, you're in for a world of disappointment, because all I could think about while he was talking, in addition to the Jim Carrey thing, was the fact that he kept sniffling and wiping his nose with his thumb, possible indicators that Dr. Smith's trick for Riding the Wave might simply be to do coke.

He said something about how counting to four on your inhale and exhale is a good way to calm yourself. As he began to explain this, and didn't stop explaining it for over forty minutes, I suddenly realized that this was the entire substance of his teaching, just this breathing and counting to four. He said you should start to think of your breath like a wave, and I tried, but instead I felt wave after wave of shock that this is where I was, in this small room in Arizona with this potentially coked-out man.

At the exact same time that I was sitting with Dr. Smith, Becky was having a private session with Tejpal, who was telling her that in a past life she had been an Irish boy.

DAY THREE

The final morning of the trip, I left my room just before six to watch Becky do the Leap of Faith. Sadly, the other development since we'd watched the *Oprah* episode those many years ago was a labral tear in my hip, making Leap of Faithing impossible (although now that it was in front of me, I was stoked to have an excuse to opt out). The name had been changed, for no reason we could discern, to the Quantum Leap. We met up with six other women in the lobby, who, in combination with Becky and me, were a perfect Breakfast Club of diversity. Among them: the fun Southern gal from Little Rock; a type A lesbian; and a kooky former surgeon with a limp, along with a few others. The guide/facilitator, Matt, was the type of guy that in New York City would be considered a unicorn: comfortable, open, nurturing, and happy to be in cargo shorts and a loose T-shirt with a name tag pinned to it.

We embarked on the five-minute walk to the obstacle area. Once again, the weather was perfect: a cloudless desert blue sky, the early-morning sun lighting all the nature around us with an electrically bright outline. Upon arriving in the shadow of the pole, we sat in a circle of white plastic chairs under a little tent and Matt asked each leaper what her intention was in doing this exercise. All of the women talked about wanting to face a fear or to leave behind an anxiety. Many mentioned wanting to be comfortable with not being in control. Susan, the one with the limp, talked about struggling with the physical challenges of her body and wanting to find peace. Another talked about going through a divorce.

As each one spoke, I felt myself, for the first time, wholeheartedly believing in this. I'd spent most of my adult life getting paid to be funny, which had often translated to looking for holes in other people's beliefs. And since I'd arrived in Tucson, I'd been reluctant to simply give in to this level of sincerity. I was haunted by the notion that, after all, wasn't this place just oozing with the worst kind of New Age bullshit? Weren't we all indulging in the most excessive kind of privilege, paying through the nose to travel here so we could talk about our itsy-bitsy feelings in our premium spandex?

But in this moment, I let go. It felt clear that everyone was both struggling and trying, stuck in the mud and also wanting out. Yes, this ritual felt silly, but it wasn't really any different from all the other ancient rituals in the world that have been created to make people feel less afraid. And so I found myself feeling compassion for the story of each of these strangers, feeling my heart pound for them as they climbed the pole as much as it pounded for Becky, who went first. When she made her way to the top, she discovered that the disk at the pole's peak both wobbled and spun. Everyone gasped as she put down one knee on the disk, and then a foot, and then found her way to standing. "How do you feel?" Matt yelled up at her. "I feel good," she shouted back. "Whenever you're ready," Matt said. Becky held on to her rope and took the leap of faith into the desert air. At the peak of her arc her rope tightened, as her peers belayed her gently down. When Becky returned to earth, everyone hugged. I took photos of each woman's turn and whooped for each. The hugging continued. I felt alive. I felt the possibility of going forward and facing life's unexpected obstacles with courage. Essentially, I felt like Oprah.

This feeling continued through dinner and afterward, when Becky, her mother, and I went to sit around the spa's fire pit. Becky was planning, per Tejpal's instructions, to write down all her life's disappointments on a piece of paper and then burn it, never mentioning them again. A few other women holding spa tea and dressed in robes were enjoying the stars. It was a scene of perfect peace, a beautifully calm night, until I heard Becky's mother say, "Oh, okay, just watch out." "What?" I said. "It's a tarantula," she said.

And sure enough, along the base of the wall not seven feet from us, I saw it, crawling in ghastly slow motion like a disembodied hand from a B-movie. I had never seen a tarantula in person before, my experience being limited to that episode of *The Brady Bunch* where the Bradys are cursed in Hawaii and Peter wakes up to find a hairy spider crawling on his chest. I remembered watching it as a kid and wondering how the actor playing Peter could have possibly dealt with something so unbearable. And I thought of how stupid I'd been to think that a few days of scribbling down aphorisms would exorcise the presence of fear from my life. The fear that my marriage would end the way my first real relationship had, with me screaming like a tortured harpy on the street. The fear that my hip injury was the beginning of a physical decline that was inevitable anyway, with my fortieth birthday looming. The fear of losing my desirability. The fear of having children, the fear of not having children. The fear of the end of the world. But mainly I thought, as I screamed and jumped onto my chair, of how insane it was that I could have ever forgotten that Arizona is filled with tarantulas, and that they'd been around me the entire time.

Ma'am

Like all women, I started out life as a miss.

When I was a little girl, people would sometimes call me miss, but in a way that was kind of playful and silly because I was just a child.

Then in my early tweens, I moved into a category at department stores called "Junior Miss," which is basically for girls who don't have breasts yet.

And then once I was a full-on teenager, I was to the world at large just miss.

"How can I help you, miss?"

"Miss, you dropped a dollar."

"Miss, can I buy you a drink?"

"Excuse me, miss, I'm interested in having sex with you."

The last one is the most important thing about being a miss. Being a miss means you are just a slip of a thing, a nymph, slim-hipped and flat-stomached and sexually alluring. Even if you're obese, if you're still a miss, you're golden.

Everyone wants a piece of a miss. Miss sounds like you're mostly air, like your body has the magic and delicacy of a wind chime and when you walk down the street everyone around you hears little bells.

Then one day everything changes.

I don't remember the exact place or time I was first called ma'am. That's abnormal for me because I tend to remember the details of traumatic things (where I was when I was first stung by a bee, the friend's house I was at when I watched the disappointing finale of *Seinfeld*). Which means on some level, I must have blocked it out.

I know I was around thirty. In my mind, I was still wind-chiming around town as a miss. And then some waiter, or maybe it was a teller at a bank, looked me up and down and decided I was a ma'am. I didn't expect to be called ma'am any more than I expected Clive Owen to walk in and demand we have sex (although in my head there might still have been a chance because again, I thought I was a miss and when you're a miss there's a very real possibility anyone at any given moment wants to fuck you, including celebrities).

In that moment I felt very viscerally the beginning of something slipping away: not just the possibility of fucking Clive Owen, but something bigger—my image of myself. How was I being perceived as a ma'am? And by how, I mean why? And just what is a ma'am anyway? And why was I so *upset*?

Ma'am makes us crazy for a bunch of reasons:

1. *Ma'am* is yet another horrible-sounding word in the lexicon of words that women are stuck with to describe various aspects of their body/life/mental state/hair. Vagina. Moist. Fallopian tubes. Yeast infection. Clitoris. Frizz. These are all terrible words, and yet they are our assigned descriptors. Who made up these words? Women certainly didn't. If, at the beginning of time, right after making vaginas, God had asked me, "What would you like your most intimate and enjoyable part of yourself to be called?," I most certainly wouldn't have said, "Vagina." No woman would, because *vagina* sounds like a First World War term that was invented to describe a trench that has been mostly blown apart but is still in use. Even off the very top of my head I feel like I could have come up with something better, like for instance the word *papoose*, which actually as I'm typing it feels like an incredibly brilliant word for a vagina.

   But ma'am fits right into this pattern. Ma'am is the onomatopoeia of drowning in a lake-size bowl of borscht. Ma'am sounds like a species of frog that just watches reality television all day. Ma'am sounds like a woman whose body is mostly cheese whiz.

2. *Ma'am* isn't just a form of address. It's a way for a perfect stranger to let us know how old he thinks we are. What is the purpose of this? Why does a

clerk at West Elm have to let me know he thinks he knows how old I am? And for the record: I am not someone who cares about hiding my age. As I'm typing this I'm thirty-nine and by the time this book is in anyone's hands I will be at the very least forty and maybe even forty-one and if you wait just a few more years to read it I will probably be mainlining Boniva. The issue isn't my comfort with my age so much as it's the why why why the fuck why does this need to be a factor in every interaction I have? Why do we have to be a nation divided between misses and ma'ams? Why do I have to be trained to respond to a different name once the world at large has decided I am no longer a fawn? I guess fawns deal with the same thing. A fawn is a fawn until one day she's checking in for a flight to Burbank at JetBlue and the TSA agent calls her doe. But I would rather be a doe than a ma'am.

3. *Ma'am* is doubly insulting because we hear men being called sir all day. And sir is awesome. We long for sir. Sir is what knights are and what Paul McCartney is. Sir sounds like you are sitting at a castle round table eating a rack of lamb. Sir means you are respected and maybe a little bit feared. No one fears ma'am, except in the sense that they may be worried oh no what if this ma'am starts hitting on me, then what will I do?

"Sir, your private plane is ready for boarding."

"Congratulations on becoming president of the United States, sir."

"What can I do to make sir happy today?"

Men are called sir starting from when they're old enough to be called anything, and they stay sir through old age (at which point chances are they're still fucking a miss). Men don't have to deal with the fact that at some point in their early midlife, they will find themselves tossed into a linguistic system that will let them know, in no uncertain terms, that in the eyes of the world, essentially, they've begun to die. When you're called sir, you're being called the same thing that James Bond is called.

For a lot of guys, being called sir is the closest they'll ever get to being an actual man.

When I'm called ma'am, I'm being called the same thing that Senator Barbara Boxer is being called, and she's seventy-five. Except scratch that. Even she famously got bent out of shape when she was addressed on the Senate floor as ma'am. She corrected the person, firmly asking to be called Senator instead of ma'am.

But if you're not a senator, and have no plans to be one, and probably couldn't be even if you wanted to because of some unfortunate YouTube videos where you do stand-up about your sex life, what do you ask to be called? We've never come up with a good alternative. But I know you can't complain if you're not trying to solve the problem yourself. So, may I offer:

Your Highness
Meryl
Khaleesi
Queen
Miss Jackson (if you're nasty)[1]

Since that first ma'am, I have now been called ma'am more times than I care to count. Once in a blue moon, I am still called miss. It's like being carded, except way better, because in the instance when someone cards me it's either because even though they know I'm of age they have to do it by law, or they're just being terribly condescending. In either case, we do the little song and dance where they ask to see ID, even though it's clear that I have no first rodeos left. Then they wait for me to say, "Ohmigod, really? Wow I haven't been carded in forever, THANK YOU." I hate saying it but it's inevitable I will say it. I don't know how to stop saying it. The farce of being asked to prove I'm not eighteen is so ridiculous that it feels like someone needs to acknowledge the ocean of bullshit we are suddenly standing in.

But someone calling me miss means maybe they still see a little of my former missy self underneath my non-skinny jeans and my glasses and the wiry white hairs sprouting from around my forehead. I do still have de-

---

1 You will probably only get that reference if you're old enough to be a ma'am.

cent boobs and thin arms and I've never smoked. And when I'm called miss, I feel an uncomfortable little thrill. Because as much as I hate to admit it, I miss the sound of that light wind-chimey word. It's embarrassing to care what someone calls me, because the number one symptom of being old is caring whether someone thinks you're old.

But the truth is—sometimes I do miss miss.

But there are also things I don't miss about being miss.

I don't miss being so vulnerable. I don't miss not knowing anything about anything. I don't miss not knowing it's better to have your clothes tailored. I don't miss people talking to me like I'm a full-on idiot, even though I often deserved it, because that's pretty much what I was. I don't miss not being able to see the most obvious red flags that silly narcissistic men were waving.

I don't miss feeling so horribly unsure about what my path should be in life and feeling deathly afraid of what making the wrong turn might mean. I didn't decide to take a leap with my life until I was thirty. I threw away a boyfriend and a steady job and my parents' way of life and went after what I wanted.

It was right when I turned into a ma'am that I finally put up my dukes.

How I Became a Comedian

1. JOAN

The thing I am sitting down to write, I started trying to write the day after Joan Rivers died. Not to get all meta on you, but I'd had some good momentum writing and then I got a little stuck and started doing the kinds of things you do when you're avoiding writing, like looking at bags online. The avoidance of writing, like the avoidance of most things, is almost always about fear. (Okay, to be honest, even in the middle of writing that sentence I looked at a bag again.)

I felt it but didn't want to admit it. I was feeling afraid. And then Joan Rivers died.

It had seemed for a few days like this might be coming, so it wasn't a shock in that sense. What was shocking to me was how much I cried when I found out. It felt like the death of a friend whom you haven't spoken with in a long time, but who always feels close.

I never got to meet Joan Rivers, but I adored her. I

adored her because she was such a badass, and because she was a woman in comedy before there were enough women in comedy for anyone to bother counting them. I adored her because once you see *A Piece of Work*, the documentary about her life, it's pretty much impossible not to love her. You see her filing her jokes on index cards in an enormous metal cabinet that spans a hallway of her hard-earned Upper East Side Versailles-style mansion and you think, *I need to work harder, because this seventy-something lady is lapping me by the minute.*

I saw her perform live once, about eight years ago, when I was living in Los Angeles. She was a force. Dressed in black pants and a black tunic and some blingy scarf/boa accessory, she was onstage at least ninety minutes, if not more. And I remember that words kept pouring out of her, with force and lust. Her performance was the difference between banging on a typewriter and pecking at a keyboard. It was all forward decisiveness, and no going back, no hesitation. Fearless.

When I tell people I do stand-up, they often say to me, "You must be so brave," but that's not really true. What bravery exists is sort of a secondary symptom to an underlying problem: desperate, aching need. In fact, I am so *not* brave that it took me years and years of therapy and arguing with myself and justifying why I was not doing stand-up, to try stand-up. Over the course of more than a decade, it is performing that has led me to possess some small amount of bravery, not the other way around. Which is why Joan's utter fearlessness is so inspiring to me.

Every now and then some person younger than me wants to talk to me about how I became a comedian. So here it is.

2. GROUCHO

At age nine, I saw *Duck Soup* on TV. The Marx Brothers' movies used to pop up occasionally on late-night PBS, back when we had a television that still required you to get up to manually turn the channels. I had a love-at-first-sight thing with Groucho. I felt like somehow he was the male me, or that I was perhaps the female him. In either case, an outside observer would strain to see a similarity (although in a few years I would grow a little mustache); I was shy and quiet with no friends. But Groucho was constantly lobbing sarcastic asides and witty observations into the air, to no one in particular, and I thought: *This is what I do all the time, but in my head, thinking these things to no one.* I watched *Animal Crackers*, *The Cocoanuts*, *A Day at the Races*, and even the movies considered lesser works because they featured the unfortunate Zeppo, who was clearly kind of glomming on.

At that time, the atmosphere of our family dinner table was always somewhat strained. Even on the evenings when we started out on a good foot, some little nick would always cut into the good feelings by the end; a rude comment from my tired, frustrated father to my tired, sweet mother; my little sister's refusal to eat her food without a Kermit puppet goading her on; my older brother, increasingly withdrawn, burying his nose in a sci-fi paperback, tucking one side of it under his plate and holding the other side open with his hand. We were a weird group, like the Royal Tenenbaums if there was no Gwyneth and everyone had a cold.

It was in this environment that I remember, from a very early age, feeling the first little pings of need to lighten the mood. If I said something funny, my family would laugh, and the clouds might part a little bit.

When I was assigned a research paper in school, I decided to do it on the Marx Brothers. In support of my effort, my father bought me tickets to see *Groucho: A Life in Revue*, an off-Broadway show written by Groucho's son about his father's life. It was the first play I ever attended. I can't vouch objectively for its quality, because to young me, it was the most important and greatest piece of art ever made. There was a scene at the end, which now would probably strike me as horrible schmaltz, in which "old Groucho" is being interviewed by a journalist, who asks, "Have you ever known sadness?" or something like that, and Groucho replies, "If I didn't know what sad was, why would I spend my whole life trying to make people laugh?" My head exploded. It felt like everything made sense. I was trying to be funny because I was sad. Groucho and I really were the same. Yes yes yes. Yay, sad!

3. YOU'RE FUNNY

In high school, after a brief friend-making renaissance at a small junior high, I once again struggled to connect with anyone. For four years, my Saturday nights ended with me alone, obsessively watching *SNL* on an old black-and-white TV I had dragged upstairs when a neighbor left it in the front entrance to be thrown away. Every day at school, I would walk past the cool kids, who were smoking and laughing on stoops right near the school entrance so the uncooler kids could see them and then they could be seen not seeing us. The alpha among them was a redhead named Masha, whose parents were from Russia and who had a cute Soviet hippie vibe, in jeans and old flannels and vintage wool Russian scarves. She was the sophisticated high school version of Charlie Brown's Little Red-Haired Girl, while I looked like Marcie, but gayer.

I never said a word to her until senior year, when we ended up in the same painting class in a cramped room where all our easels were jammed up against one another. I was a good artist, a little morsel of identity that had never gotten exposure during my torturous four years at this math and science high school. We were doing self-portraits, and I was painting a decent representation of my body dysmorphia. I was next to Masha, who'd been chatting for half a semester with every other girl in her proximity but me. Then, as I added delicate blue under-eye circles to my hawk-nosed image, she suddenly took notice. "That's really good," she said, breaking the ice as casually as if she'd been tapping open a crème brûlée. From that moment forward, I was welcomed into the circle of Masha's art period chat. Maybe it was because we were just a few months from graduating and I knew pretty soon Masha's judgment of my life would be meaningless; but whatever the reason, I opened up and relaxed and was some semblance of myself. I made sarcastic asides and witty observations, like Groucho, out loud.

A month or two into class, Masha turned to me and, with the confidence of someone used to being the last word on others' value, said, "You're funny." She said it the same way she'd said my painting was good, like it was a discovery she had made that was worthy of announcement. Like she was sticking an American flag in the moon. And it meant everything to me. Masha thought I was funny. I was a funny person. I had given up on competing for pretty. But funny felt like uncharted territory where there was a lot of land up for grabs.

4. AM I DYING PART 1

I was accepted to Vassar College. It was the school where my father wanted me to go[1] so I obediently applied and was accepted. I graduated high school in June and teetered across the stage with the rest of my class at

---

1   I think he was enamored of the class implied by the "Vassar girl" image as well as the 70:30 female-to-male ratio.

Lincoln Center, wearing an off-brand Laura Ashley–esque dress and heeled leather ankle boots that I had no idea how to walk in. I have a memory of my mother telling me that I was walking like a transvestite on their very first day in women's shoes, but it seems impossible my eternally sweet and kind mother would say that. That said, it was an accurate description.

Early in July, I woke up to a dull ache in the center of my pelvis. I waited a few days for it to pass, but it remained, steady. More upsetting than the level of pain was its location. Although I was a virgin who knew nothing about my own anatomy, I decided that I most likely had cervical cancer and was going to die before I left for college. The tragedy of it, of my parents having sacrificed everything to be able to get me to this point, and then me rudely expiring before they could see their dreams realized through me, was too much to bear.

I finally told my mother about the pain I was having, and after asking me if I always made sure to wash my vagina with soap (I didn't, usually water only) she took me to a gynecologist at a city hospital. My parents, both city employees, had excellent insurance that would have allowed us to see a private doctor, so I'm not sure why she chose an underfunded government institution for my very first gynecological exam, but that is what she did. I remember sitting in a sad dirty plastic chair with the nurse as she filled out my paperwork. When she asked me if I was sexually active, I answered truthfully, no. She looked at me. I was seventeen. "C'mon, seriously?" she said. I was being reverse slut-shamed. There were so few virginal seventeen-year-old girls in New York City that she literally did not believe me.

The exam went badly. The doctor was as much of a husk as the nurse. I remember lying on the table with my feet in the stirrups for the first time, terrified of someone going near my cervix. She tried to insert the speculum and every muscle below my neck went into shutdown mode. After wrestling with my vagina for a minute or two, she tossed her instrument on the table. "I can't do this," she said, frustrated with me for being such a virginal pain in the ass.

In pursuit of someone who could diagnose my symptoms, my mom shepherded me to a few more doctors in different fields, including a Greek neurologist with the thickest black beard I'd ever seen. Even though it was closely cropped, you could not see a centimeter of his skin. He could not figure out what was wrong with me, either.

As a result of this medical mystery, I sank into a deep depression. Normally an early riser, I would lie in bed till almost noon, thinking about my impending death and the fruitlessness of beginning any endeavor. I didn't want to tell my parents I was dying, wanting to save them from this devastating news as long as possible, or at least until I was too weak to care for myself. Suffering with this news alone was often more than I felt I could bear. Twenty-two years later, I still remember one sunny morning when the depth of my sadness had me wanting to writhe out of my own skin. Since that was impossible, I got out of bed, went to our bathroom, and crawled into the dry bathtub, where I curled into the fetal position and cried silently in my pajamas.

I took to lying in my parents' bed (which also served as our family's couch) during the day while they were at work, and watching Comedy Central. At the time, their programming was still a heavy serving of Benny Hill reruns, punctuated by long stretches of back-to-back stand-up specials. I watched the stand-up. The shows were filled with all the emerging greats of the 1990s— Louis CK, Chris Rock, Paula Poundstone, Elayne Boosler, and, most inspiring to my seventeen-year-old mind, a young Janeane Garofalo in tights and pajama shorts standing onstage with a notebook. I wanted to be her friend, and more than that, I also felt a vague stirring of wanting to just be her. Under the covers, still in a ball, I would smile and occasionally laugh out loud at the TV. Watching them became a comfort, like being curled up next to a fire. I felt a growing warmth, a leaning toward the light. Maybe I would live to go to college. Maybe I could just make it through freshman year, before succumbing to my imaginary illness.

5. AM I DYING PART 2

My freshman year in college, I tried out for the school's popular sketch comedy troupe, the atrociously named

Laughingstock. I had to write a sketch that the group would read and perform with me during the audition, and I came up with something about a blind mime. I recall nothing about it except how funny I thought it was when I wrote it and how certainly I would die of shame if anyone were to see it now. Still, when I went to go peek at the paper that was posted the next day with the names of the four new accepted members, mine was one of them.

I had never been onstage before in any capacity. A few weeks before the show, we got access to rehearse in the black-box theater where we would actually perform. I can still remember the smell of the space, a dark smoky smell of wood and handsaws. I felt like I was now in that sacred inner sanctum of theater kids; you know (theater kids are the same everywhere), the kids who would sit in a tight circle on the grass or sing really loud in the middle of a crowded room or cry in public, tears falling down their beautiful cheeks and landing on an artfully knotted scarf.

A few days before the show, I was lying on my narrow dorm bed (which was on the floor, natch), reading Nietzsche (natch again) when I started to feel sick. My head hurt. Then my vision began to blur. I was overcome by nausea. And then, something scarier than any of the other things happened: My right arm went completely numb, from my shoulder all the way to my fingers. I tried to grab my coat off a hook on my door and found I couldn't lift my arm. I ran to the campus medical center, where the night nurse hugged me while I cried that something was horribly wrong. As we talked, the feeling in my arm returned. After half an hour of observation, we decided I was okay. I was given some juice and sent back to my room.

But then it happened again, the morning after our next rehearsal. This time, I woke up to a headache so excruciating that I immediately projectile-vomited all over the room. In a moment of perfect irony, the vomit landed on my copy of Nietzsche's *Human, All Too Human.* I called Penny, a girl I was friends with but didn't always like, and she came over and cleaned up the vomit and wiped off Nietzsche. I felt a little guilty for knowing that Penny's caretaker personality would not allow her to refuse helping me, but I was also glad my puke was gone.

This pattern of headaches accompanied by vision problems, throwing up, and bodily numbness was eventually diagnosed by the campus doctor as a series of migraine headaches, but not before I had to go home to Manhattan and get an MRI to rule out a brain tumor, which meant that for two weeks, as I rehearsed my first-ever comedy show, I was convinced, once again, that I was dying.

What was confusing about the sickness I'd been experiencing, to both me and the doctors, was I had absolutely no history of headaches whatsoever, and since that moment in college, I have never, ever had them again.

I was well enough to perform in the show. The moment

I got my very first laugh, performing in a sketch I'd written about being a bad sport playing chess (wherein I got to knock pieces off a chess set over and over), I felt a wave of pleasure wash over me. And with the pleasure came an enormous fear. In retrospect, it's clear to me that the headaches were a symptom of a reptilian terror I wasn't even aware I had: a terror of finally taking a step toward knowing that what I wanted to do with my life was this uncertain, impossible career, completely unlike the previous things I, or my father, had ever dared to imagine for me.

6. SURF REALITY

After college, unsure of what to do, I turned to my boyfriend Pete, who pointed me toward a temp agency called "Force One." Force One was run by a mustachioed man named Jeff, who'd carved out a temping niche placing people at entertainment companies. It was the only temp agency in New York where you did not have to take a typing test or a Microsoft Office proficiency test, both of which I had failed at other agencies. At Force One, the only screening tool was an interview with Jeff, who would shoot the shit with you until he decided he liked you, at which point he'd ask where you wanted to work. I told Jeff I wanted to work at Comedy Central, and, after a brief assignment at Turner Publicity, where my sole task in two weeks was to call Asia de Cuba to inquire if my boss (a poor man's Téa Leoni) had left a mink stole there, Jeff called to tell me he had a placement for me at my first choice.

I started temping for a woman in human resources who was herself responsible for calling in temps. I often described the meta-ness of this situation to my friends as similar to when you see a dog holding its leash in its own mouth, so as to walk itself. One afternoon, people from the development department called to say they'd just fired their assistant and needed a temp. In full "I'll pay the rent!" hero mode, I requested a switch, took the elevator two floors up, and started a job I would stay at for the next seven years.

Working at Comedy Central was like college, except a million times more awesome and I was paid for it. I was in a small department where I worked for two people, one in talent and one in programming development. They were both fun and we'd do the sorts of things people do at fun jobs: going for naughtily long lunches, taking dirty quizzes on the (primitive) Internet to find out if we were perverts, and expensing the decadent dinners we'd have before going to stand-up shows. I read scripts that came bound in fancy agency binders, from CAA and UTA and William Morris. I felt like anyone who wrote anything that was bound in an agency binder was impossibly important.

Eventually I was promoted, and then promoted again. I sat with Robert Smigel as he pitched *TV Funhouse.* I accompanied my boss to meetings with Stephen Colbert and Amy Sedaris as they conceived episodes of *Strangers with Candy.* I brought coffee to a young Amy Poehler and Matt Walsh and Ian Roberts and Matt Besser as they worked on their new Upright Citizens Brigade sketch show. I could not believe this was my life.

But time passed and I started getting used to this being my life, and the more used to it I got, the more I felt small but insistent pangs of wonder about the lives of all the creative people I was meeting, and how they'd gotten to where they were. How were they raised so they could just wake up and do these incredibly free and creative and wild things every day? Did they go to the college their father told them to go to? I spent so many nights sitting in the back of these incredible alt stand-up shows, and in particular a place called Luna Lounge, a dive bar on Ludlow Street with an even divier performance space in the back, which has since been replaced by either a macaron store or a soulless glass condo, or some combination thereof. There I watched many of the same people perform live whom I used to watch on TV while I was dying of fake cervical cancer. I fell into an emotional pattern wherein on nights I saw an amazing comedian perform, I'd feel this longing that this was something I wanted to try; and on nights I saw an amateur flailing, I'd think, *Well, I can at least be this bad, right?*

This back-and-forth went on in my head for months, and then years. The fear of trying stand-up and the fear of not trying stand-up were locked in an endless stalemate, where both sides made convincing arguments and both sides agreed it would be a good idea if instead of making a decision I just sat on the floor of the crap apartment Pete and I shared and ordered huge amounts of truly terrible Indian food.

But then one night my friend Wendy, who had started taking a stand-up class, told me about an open-mike night where the pressure to have talent was so low as to be nonexistent. She took me to scope out the venue, a place called Surf Reality a block down from Luna Lounge (it is also no longer in existence; I think it has been replaced by one of those mysterious boutiques that just has one $4,000 T-shirt hanging in the window).

Surf Reality was even grimier than Luna Lounge, a hipster lean-to where the black linoleum floor was permanently shellacked with a sticky film of beer. The open mike was run by a waify woman named Reverend Jen who wore elf ears. Her system was that you paid $3 up front, and then you'd put your name on a piece of paper into a jar and wait for it to be pulled out, at which point an egg timer would be set to exactly five minutes, during which you could do whatever you wanted. The attendees of this particular open mike took the free-for-all quality of this very seriously. Perhaps because Reverend Jen insisted that every performance be greeted only with positivity, all kinds of psychopathic navel-gazing was permitted. There was an enormous guy called Little Bill who looked like a murderous Bruce Vilanch, who wore all black save for two giant yellow flashlights tucked into his belt and carried a Polaroid camera that he would stick in your face and snap without asking. His time onstage would always be spent scream-reading from a terrifying spiral notebook filled with his sociopathically tiny handwriting. There was a woman who would read poems about her father and always be crying by the end. That kind of thing.

After a few weeks in a row of watching Little Bill primal-scream, I decided that Wendy was right, and even in the event that my jokes did not kill, I would be okay with it since it was mostly an elf-ear kind of crowd and I would never have to see them again. I typed up seven jokes word-for-word and carried the paper in my pocket. I remember one of my jokes was about the subway and how scary it is when you're in the tunnel and you hear your train honking. Then I'd say, "What's out there, a DEER?" All of it was very bad. I paid my $3 and then sat shivering, like a small, nervous Chihuahua, until my name was called. When it was my turn, I took the mike from Reverend Jen, a little freaked about how to raise the mike stand (something I'd been studying with great concern from afar), and, shaky hands giving away my nerves, started to read my jokes off the paper. Miraculously, the elves laughed.

7. DYING (AGAIN)

About six months after the first time I did stand-up, Pete and I broke up. Two weeks after we broke up, 9/11 happened. I thought for sure this national tragedy would bring us back together like so many other couples, but he seemed to feel he could weather this global geopolitical shift with the new girl he was fucking. I was subletting my old boss Chris's one-bedroom apartment in Brooklyn Heights, directly across from the BQE. There was a small, mauve daybed in the living room that was permanently dusted with cat hair from when Chris had lived there with three of them. In this sad little nest, I would order cheap Thai food and watch CNN on the world's smallest TV while my heartache turned my whole body into a pretzel. My walk to and from the train was long, about fourteen minutes up one of the most beautiful streets in Brooklyn, and often at night on my walk home, passing elegant brownstones with steps lit by old flame lanterns, I would sob.

One night, I was lying on the daybed when I became aware of an odd crawling sensation under the skin covering my right cheekbone, as if there were a worm squirming toward my nose. Soon I felt it on both sides. This sensation was later accompanied by a transient numbing of patches of my face. Back I went to the neurologist, to several neurologists. I memorized and passed their tests—feeling the point of a toothpick on my palms or the coldness of a little metal hammer against my cheek, following their fingers with my eyes to the right, left, and around. When we were done with the toothpicks and hammers, they would usually dismiss me as fine, which should have made me feel better but didn't. Instead I obsessed over this new illness that would take me down right when I'd lost my partner, and I would die alone, without having a boyfriend to promise, in a whisper, that he would go on and find someone else when I died, because that is what true love is and I am selfless.

In this state, I tried to adapt to the rhythms of single life and failed miserably. This was before absolutely everyone had moved to Brooklyn, and most of my friends still lived in Manhattan. I didn't know what to do when another person's movements did not provide the emotional tick-tock of the day's clock, and I would sometimes wake up and just sit on the edge of my bed staring at nothing, like a sad person on a motel bed in an arty photograph from the 1970s.

The one thing that pulled me out of bed was the growing number of stand-up shows I would do at night, primarily because there was literally nothing else on my dance card. These shows were usually in the basements of bars, or the back rooms of divey restaurants. They would start late at night and go into the wee hours of the morning, and there would inevitably be a moment where I wondered how it was possible my life had led me to sitting on a metal folding chair in a cement-block room at one in the morning while some guy in baggy jeans talked about his dick onstage. When I went up, I was so nervous that I still typed my stand-up word-for-word. But slowly, over time, I started to loosen my grip on predictability. I carried a little spiral notebook in which I would jot one-word ideas—"catcalls"; "turkeyburgers"[2]—and I became

---

2   These both became terrible jokes, in case that isn't obvious.

comfortable with the idea that perhaps improvising just a smidge onstage was maybe okay. I transitioned from open mikes to occasionally, every now and then, doing a "booked" show, which meant someone actually invited you to perform and you were not waiting till some crazy witching hour to spew jokes at your fellow open-mikers.

One night I was booked to perform at a show I'd never done before—my understanding was that it was at the gym of an old Children's Aid Society. I didn't feel like going to tell jokes. I was miserable. I had run into Pete and his new girlfriend on the subway platform that morning, although technically it was less a "run into" than a "see them from afar, have a near heart attack, duck behind a pole, notice how he impulsively ducks in to kiss her like the love and desire he has for her is more than he can contain, think about staying because you have to get to work and this is your train, and then change your mind and simply leave the subway altogether and take a cab." It had been a gut punch, and all I wanted to do was lie on my daybed couch and breathe in cat hair. But I still had enough type A college student left in me that I couldn't make a commitment to tell jokes at a gym and not show up, so somehow I pulled myself together and got on the train.

I got to the space, expecting to perform under a ratty basketball hoop to about fifteen people. Instead, the gym was packed with hundreds of guests. People were sitting at cocktail tables with candles on them, like actual human beings instead of just random bar-goers who'd been roped into a comedy show while waiting on line for a piss. My stomach flipped, and for the first time in months it wasn't because of something I heard Pete did, but because I had never performed in front of this many people before. And the other comedians on the bill were all real comics, people I'd gone to see for my job and whom I respected.

I got onstage and talked. I talked about my life. It was, up to that moment, the best I had ever done. I killed. I got offstage and I did not feel like someone with worms crawling under her eye socket.

I felt alive.

8. BEST WEEK EVER

I was still working at Comedy Central during the day and then doing stand-up at night. I was doing well sometimes and bombing other times, but I felt I was finding something, and that something was pushing me along. One day I got a call from a producer I'd met who was starting a new show at VH1 called *Best Week Ever*. It would be a topical "talking head" show where comics would riff on pop-culture events of the week. He'd seen me do stand-up and wanted to talk to me about being on it. *HOLY FUCK I AM GOING TO BE ON TV*, I thought to myself.

Being on *Best Week Ever* meant that the night before shooting, the producers would email me a packet of over a hundred questions regarding celeb news from the week, with the idea being that you would write jokes as answers to all of the questions. There would always be a lot of questions about Britney Spears's vagina or Lindsay Lohan's boobs. I would dutifully try to come up with at least one joke per question. Often I would wake up at five thirty in the morning to finish writing, sprawling on my bed hungover.

Because I had a day job, they accommodated me by always shooting me first thing in the morning, which usually meant arriving at VH1 around eight a.m. I would go into hair and makeup, talk about Lindsay's pussy for an hour, then do my best to rub off my full face of makeup before literally running the ten blocks back up Broadway to Comedy Central, where my boss, the endlessly patient Lou Wallach, would pretend not to notice that his normally plain-faced and bedraggled employee had mascara all over her eyes and clearly had had her hair done into professionally beachy waves.

Best Week Ever was the first time I was on TV. People talk about getting "big breaks"—this was the teensiest, it-siest, bitsiest of breaks. Aside from getting trolled online for my appearance, people saw me. I was getting paid. It made up for the fact that I was at a period in my domestic life where one morning I made eggs for breakfast, and then was too emotionally checked out to do dishes for a while. When I finally went over to the sink after a few days, I lifted a plate to reveal a nest of newly born maggots, squiggling all over my dirty dishes and in between the tines of my forks.

9. THE LEAP, THEN INFINITE LEAPS

I lived a double life for more than a year, being at my job by day, and then doing stand-up at night, with occasional early-morning forays into appearing on TV. The quiet little twinge I had felt years before, that maybe what I wanted to do was this unstable and risky thing, was growing louder. I tried to ignore it, the same way I'd tried for years to ignore the call to do stand-up at all. My father had raised me to avoid risk at all costs—his attempt to save us from the fate of his own father, a gambler whose favorite stakes always seemed to be the well-being and stability of his family (and who lost, in spectacular ways, over and over).

One day I got a call from the head writers of the *Late Show with David Letterman.* They'd seen me on TV and wanted me to submit a writing packet to be considered for a staff writer job. This was a mind-blowing inquiry, seeing as how David Letterman was probably my second biggest comedy crush after Groucho and as a ten-year-old girl I'd had fantasies about meeting him at a party, falling in love, and marrying him. I worked on the packet for weeks, staying at my office till midnight to use the printer, before I finally dropped it off by hand at the Ed Sullivan Theater. I didn't hear anything for months and forgot about it.

Then one day the phone rang. They wanted me. I would be hired on a thirteen-week contract, which would be renewed for another thirteen weeks if I was doing a good job. This is a standard offer for entry-level television writing.

That night I went to my parents' house to tell them the good news. My mom was excited, but my father was dubious. He was not a big Letterman fan. Comedically, his taste runs more toward Lenny Bruce. Then I made the mistake of mentioning the thirteen-week contract.

"Thirteen weeks? And then they can just drop ya?" he asked.

"I guess hypothetically, yes."

And then he said, "Well, that doesn't sound like much of a job at all."

And as soon as I heard that, even though I wrestled with it a few more days, I knew I wouldn't take the offer from Letterman.

I hated myself for not taking it. In the days after I sheepishly called to politely decline, my stomach was in a constant knot. But this time I didn't think I had cancer, or an appendix that was about to explode. Unlike all the previous moments in my life when a vague illness would present itself as a kind of physical resistance to the option of growing, of changing, this time my body stayed mum. It was not going to provide me with a distraction from looking into the unknown and having a very serious conversation with myself about why I was pussing out on what I wanted to do. I knew that I was the problem.

When the next offer came, I took it: an offer to write on a show in LA. But it was a year later. It took me that full year to gather my confidence enough to leave.

And this is where I come back to Joan, and why she matters so much to me. I saw an interview with her once where she talked about why she felt she was doing her best work at seventy-one years old. "Because I'm not scared anymore," she said. "There's nothing they can do to me. They've already done all of it. I've been through everything and I just have no fear." I thought of these words recently, clung to them actually, as I sat in a hotel room in Los Angeles. I was in the middle of a series of pitch meetings to try to sell a television show. These meetings, for me anyway, are always fraught with the potential for serious self-loathing. You go from network to network, get offered water by an assistant, take the water, and then do your song and dance about yourself and why your story matters to a room full of often bored, and occasionally boring, executives.

I'd just finished my first meeting and was starting to spiral out about how it went. Hearing myself speaking my ideas out loud had suddenly felt embarrassing. And now I was stewing in my hotel room, forecasting my rejection. But then I thought of Joan, who'd just died a few days before. I thought about how she refused to die before she was dead. I thought about how often throughout my life I'd gone into a deep depression about my imagined imminent death. And it occurred to me that imagining death must have been to me on some level less frightening than imagining living—i.e., going forward into this risky, terrifying unknown despite the possibility of failure.

I thought about Joan, and thought about my fear of

telling my story and having no one care, and then I thought, *Fuck it. I care. I don't care if they care. It's my story.* I relaxed and ordered an unnecessary amount of room service before driving to my next meeting.

They bought it.

Dogshit

You watch the Emmys and the Oscars your whole life and you think, Oh, this is so glamorous I want to be a PRINZESS like all these other ladies. Oh, if only I could just walk the red carpet. Oh if only I could just be asked who I am wearing and put my mani in the mani cam and have Ryan Seacrest tell me I look beautiful. I want someone to do my hair so it looks like I just floated across the ocean to Los Angeles via a giant shell. I want to be spray-tanned until I am the color of a just-baked Chips Ahoy cookie, like JLo. I want Giuliana Rancic to ask me how are you in that way where she implies we are friends even though we are not friends. I want to be dripping in sequins and pose with one foot delicately placed in front of the other like I am a perfect little female pony. A golden palomino pony trotting up to the stage to get my golden trophy. Then I would feel amazing, like I am special and an angel, and not be haunted by this frequent feeling that in comparison with them, with the

Prinzezzes on the red carpet and in magazines and on billboards, I am dogshit.

These are the feelings I always felt. Then I was nominated for an Emmy.

When we found out we were nominated for best sketch show and best variety writing, for *Inside Amy Schumer*, we all freaked. Not only did we just finish a critically acclaimed third season, but Amy's movie *Trainwreck* had come out over the summer, and she had become very very famous.

Truth be told, we'd been nominated for writing the year prior, but due to a tangle of boring rules, our category's award was presented during what are called the "Creative Arts Emmys," which are held the week before the "real" Emmys and are untelevised. The categories are primarily technical, as evidenced by the number of awards we watched being given to the editors of the reality show *Deadliest Catch*. The ceremony is usually hosted by some hot B-level actress, who is thrown as a kind of ironic bone to the nominees to apologize for the fact that they themselves are too unfuckable to put on TV. So even though I'd technically been an Emmy nominee the year before, I'd still felt like dogshit. And we lost, which sealed the dogshit feeling.

But this year we are nominated for the real televised Emmys. Yay! We are not dogshit anymore. We are going to be Prinzessez.

I, however, have one major curveball in all this, which is, I am twelve weeks out from having given birth. You might be saying wait, what? You didn't tell me you were pregnant. Well, that's how long it takes to write a book. I wasn't pregnant when I started writing it. Now I have a baby. More on that later. The point is, at the time I'm going to go buy my dress for the televised cool-people Emmys, I am still thirty pounds overweight and I basically have the body of a bodega honey bear. Even my feet have gone up a size. So the Prinzezz fantasy is already facing a major obstacle.

A month before the ceremony, I hand the baby to Mike and run top speed out the door to Bergdorf Goodman, because I only have a few hours before I have to return home to ~~milk myself~~ pump. In my head I'm picturing that perhaps I can wear some kind of gauzy, tent-like dress. I'd seen something online in this vein that I thought might work, and texted the picture to a friend, who immediately responded "u can't go to the Emmys looking like Mrs. Roper." I was bummed because I'd really been relying on that look.

At Bergdorf, I grab a few of the most promising-looking tents and try them on. Even in the largest sizes, nothing is fitting correctly. I look around the floor for a salesperson with a gentle aura and land on a delight of a woman named Jennifer. (Jennifer, if you are reading this, yes you are a DELIGHT.) I explain to Jennifer that I am nominated for an Emmy and this is my chance to be a Prinzezz, but I'm post-baby and I have the body of a mozzarella ball. Jennifer finds a short black dress with a fringe cape that drapes across the front so my newly formed fupa (Google it) is hidden from view. Somehow, it looks kind of great. I cannot believe I have been able to find a dress in under two hours (see: wedding dress chapter) but moreover I am giddy that my red carpet fantasy is back on track. I briefly get nervous about the fact that the dress is too short to be appropriate for a black-tie event, but then I Google "short Emmy dress" and see that Julia Roberts once wore a knee-length dress to the Emmys. *If Julia can do it, I can do it*, I think to myself, even though that is 100 percent not a true thing to think and actually the opposite is true.

Still, I am amped to walk the red carpet. At Saks I buy a pair of satin Manolo Blahnik shoes with a Swarovski crystal swoosh along the arch. My friend, who has come along as my shoe wingwoman, takes a picture of me holding the shoe box with the MANOLO label, as if I am a tourist standing in front of a local landmark, which in some sense I am: I am a tourist in the land of aspirational footwear that costs as much as I used to pay in monthly rent. I have no plans to move here, but I am enjoying a vacation from my country, the land of Toms.

I fly to Los Angeles. The network is paying for me to fly business class, so the Prinzezz feeling is off to a good start. As I drink my pre-takeoff champagne and adjust my seat into a bed (a BED!), I watch the sad Others stream past me into coach. For most of my life I have been one of them, trying to keep my head high as I walk past the smug few, sprawled out in their ample seats, their warm hand-towels already crumpled in front of them, waiting to be discreetly tonged away by the sky-help. You cannot help but hate all those people a bit, as you struggle past with your bag, waiting for your fellow hoi polloi to mash their suitcases into the overhead. But now that the tables have turned, and I am the one sitting in business class eating (free) (warm!) nuts, I can't help but feel a pang of survivor guilt. I want the people walking past me to know that I'm one of them. My ticket is being paid for by a corporation; I could not afford it on my own. In my heart I am a coach person. But if I were really a coach person, would I be feeling such joy at perusing the menu I have been handed, with choices of appetizer, entrée, and dessert, as if we were on the ground? Perhaps; but I am also aware that this joy has a shadow over it, which is the sense that I am an imposter in these big fancy loungers, and my grip on these amenities is tenuous. For the next five hours my brain vibrates between pleasure and anxiety as I contemplate my commercial flight identity. I look around to see if any of my fellow passengers are experiencing similar feelings.

Everyone is either asleep or watching Bravo.

On the ground, I carry my garment bag over my shoulder through the airport. Just carrying a garment bag feels pretty special to me. Who am I, the Queen of England?

Or maybe…

I AM A PRINZESS.

The next morning is Emmy morning. I have booked a hair and makeup artist to come "glam" me "up." The woman who appears at my door is lovely and very kindly pretends not to notice the fact that I am drinking a glass of white wine at eleven a.m. I joke, "It's eleven fifteen somewhere!" She is super nice to ignore this. When she asks if I have any thoughts on a look, I have the embarrassing task of showing her a Pinterest page I've made of celebrities with smoky eyes and side buns. I blather for about five minutes about how I do not expect her to actually make me look like Cate Blanchett. She is a champ and so she lets me splash around in my puddle of low self-esteem without telling me to chill the fuck out, which she would absolutely be within her rights to do.

Two hours later, I do not look like Cate Blanchett, but I have to admit I look nice. I look as nice as I've looked in the three months since a small boy emerged from my vagina. I am wearing my fringy dress and my crystal shoes and even sparkly clip-on earrings.[1] Also I am wearing a pretty ring that Mike bought me for my fortieth birthday. Can a Prinzezz be forty? I look in the mirror and am just starting to feel like maybe I'm pulling this off when I realize the Spanx shorts I have on over my underwear are creating a huge panty line. Prinzezzes don't have panty lines. Prinzezzes probably have perfectly smooth plastic non-genitals like Barbie. I thought the Spanx would smooth out the panty line. Now I have to consider whether these Spanx can be worn without underwear. Am I disgusting? I take off my underwear and sausage myself into the Spanx.

---

1   I do not have pierced ears because I am a pussy.

Then I begin the sad task of packing up my breast pump, which will be coming along with me to the Emmys. I have a black canvas tote bag with mesh pockets on the sides meant for holding the kind of giant steel thermoses guys from Colorado carry whenever they leave the house.

I have a pang of regret about not having purchased something fancy in which to carry the breast pump. What kind of hayseed dipshit walks the red carpet with a canvas tote bag in her hand? I had briefly considered buying something sequined and fun to use as an ad hoc pump bag, but then I felt embarrassed. Not wanting to walk the red carpet carrying a breast pump felt like the worst kind of petty vanity. Shouldn't I just be happy to be there? Am I already the kind of person who can't carry my own stuff around? Do I seriously think I'm the Queen of England?

No.

But the dirty secret is, I do want to be a Prinzezzzzz. I can't let go of the fantasy, the image of myself as one of those perfectly poised palomino ladies, every detail, every lash, in place. It's not so much that I want to look the way they look as that I want to feel the way I imagine looking that way feels. I guess this feeling would best be described as, how do you say, "deserving"—a sensation so foreign to most women that L'Oréal was able to sell one dillion lipstick tubes just by having a spokeswoman say the catchphrase, "Because you're worth it." Four words that penetrated to the core of the female mind, like Luke Skywalker's final shot that detonated the Death Star.

I panic and text a producer friend at the Emmys asking if a production assistant could maybe meet me at the entrance and take my breast pump to the designated dressing room where it's been arranged for me to pump after the show. Even though my producer friend says it's no problem, I feel like I am already a cliché—the temperamental Hollywood asshole who throws an inappropriately foamed latte at some nice young person's head. "You're being too hard on yourself," some tiny voice from within says. The self-loathing part of me throws a latte at that voice's head.

Tote bag in hand, I get into a white stretch limo with my colleagues at around two p.m. The interior is outlined with disco lights, and there's a giant decanter of brown booze, which means we are officially having Fun!

That afternoon, the temperature is hovering around a hundred degrees. We exit our car and step into the glare of the Los Angeles sun. Within seconds we are soaking in sweat. There's a short pre-red-carpet red carpet into the Staples Center, where servers are offering platters of champagne. There is also a free makeup station where a young girl of about nine is getting a touch-up. Edie Falco walks past me. EDIE FALCO.

Emmys!

By the time I find the nice young lady who is taking my breast pump from me, the champagne people have vanished and the bars have, unbelievably, closed. I'd been relying on booze to help me ignore the pain being caused by the Manolo Blahniks. (I was expecting them to be uncomfortable. We've all heard people talk about suffering for fashion, but I was not expecting them to be excruciating to the extent that even just sitting with them on—not walking or standing—is agonizing.) Oh well. I will just have water, and drink booze later. I'm parched, as most of my body's moisture evaporated on the walk from the car to the lobby.

But there is no water to be found. The Emmys seem to have run out of water bottles. I look to see if Edie Falco has any water, but she has vanished.

Oh God, please don't let Edie Falco dehydrate.

I cannot dwell on this because an announcer tells us over the loudspeaker that it is time to head to the auditorium, which means it's Walk the Red Carpet o'clock. Prinzezz Time. Fancy Go Time. Fantasy Perfect Lady Time. I am so glad I am not carrying my canvas tote. I take a deep breath and join the glittery wave of sequined and tuxedoed humanity clippity-clopping toward the doors that are being held open for us by Emmy elves. My writer colleagues and I cross the threshold and blink for a moment, blinded by the blistering sun. When I open my eyes, I see that there is a velvet rope parting the red carpet, like the sea of the same color, into two paths. To my left there is a barrier, behind which hundreds of random onlookers gawk and take photos. And to my right, illuminated by a lightning storm of camera flashes, are the celebrity nominees, flanked by their attendants.

If I had any doubt about the pecking order, it's quickly erased when I spy a friend of mine on the fancier side of the rope. We squeal and run toward each other with out-stretched arms to hug over the partition, when suddenly a giant security guard jumps in front of me and practically body-checks me to the ground. He barks at me to move along. My friend looks at me helplessly as we are forcibly parted. I'm embarrassed. I look for a bottle of water and still can't find any. My colleagues and I end up sharing one mini bottle of "Emmy"-label water that is lukewarm from the heat. We sip each other's backwash as we make our way to our seats, with security occasionally yelling at us to hurry up. I feel a familiar pit pitting around in my gut.

How is it possible I still feel like dogshit?

This was supposed to be the one moment in life that would make up for the thousands of times I looked at red carpet photos of Angelina Jolie and Cate Blanchett and even Selena Gomez at awards shows and felt like they were creatures from another planet. I've never been able to shake this niggling little masochistic compulsion to look at these images, even though they always have given me a small pang of sadness. It is the same pang I felt when I saw the movie *Amélie* and first gazed with awe at Audrey Tautou—this perfect feminine confection with her bangs and her emerald midi skirt and that perfect little bow of a mouth. For weeks afterward I had this unshakable melancholic ache whose cause I couldn't put my finger on, until I realized it was an irrational sense of loss over the fact that I would never, no matter how hard I tried, look like Amélie.

But if I were ever going to taste it, today would be the day.

Instead, having made it to this bizarre little Oz, I find that I am not on the yellow brick road but rather a parallel side street. The Emmy urban planners have created these corrals so that everyone knows exactly, and literally, where they stand. And in my case, it is between the red carpet with the Prinzezzes, who are being treated as such, and the huddled masses of fans on my left, yearning for a photograph of anyone famous. Even when I think I have reached the top, I am still stuck in the middle. My friends back home are barraging me with texts asking, "How do you feel?" and the truth is that even though of course I am grateful to be here, because I'm not a complete asshole, I am getting yelled at by a security guard. And that is disappointing. I am as close as I will ever get to the Prinzezzes, and yet I am still not one of them and in fact large professional bouncers are making sure I do not get too close. *Oh well*, I think. *Of course.*

So then once we are inside, something bananas happens: We win the Emmy for best sketch show, and suddenly I am standing on the stage looking through the television screen which I have always watched from the other side. Holyshitholyshitholyshit. In the sixty seconds we are up there, I experience a rush of discoveries. I discover that when you walk onstage at the Emmys, you start shaking uncontrollably. I discover that when you win an Emmy you are seized by the hope that all your ex-boyfriends are watching. I discover that when you exit stage right, you are ushered into a VIP lounge where there is finally (FINALLY) booze, as well as a giant stack of doughnuts and sushi.[2] Viola Davis is sitting by herself waiting for a drink. Mel Brooks is in the corner smiling and chatting with friends. I order a glass of white wine and head for the food, where LL Cool J and I both shove salmon sashimi into our mouths. The entire situation is surreal, as two thoughts jostle shoulders in my mind: (1) *I have won an Emmy*; and (2) *I don't truly belong here.*

This carousel of anxiety only halts because I look across the room and see a handsome man with an adorable smile and terrific blue eyes talking to an equally stunning woman. I am wearing contacts, so my vision is a little loopy. But this man looks familiar. I squint, squint again, and then realize, holy shit: It's Ben McKenzie.

Ben McKenzie! You know, the lead of *The O.C.*, my favorite TV show from 2003 to 2007. He played Ryan. Ryan who was from the wrong side of the tracks but whose life changes when he is taken under the wing of his public defender, Sandy, played by Peter Gallagher (Jewing it up to great effect). Sandy lives with his family in tony Newport Beach. It is the fanciest place Ryan's ever been!

It was such a fucking awesome show. My friend Kate and I were obsessed with it and watched every single week and then hopped on the phone immediately

---

2   Apparently the true reward for "making it" in Hollywood is not acclaim or even money, but simply being allowed to feel as if you finally deserve to eat, e.g., "Hey, great work on *Mad Men/Scandal/Game of Thrones*! You have earned a doughnut hole."

afterward to discuss. We would have texted but the show existed pre-texting.

I can't believe I am in the same room as RYAN!

I'm just drunk enough to know that I need a photo with him, but I am also sober enough to be worried that he'll be annoyed by this random fan asking for a picture. I am sure people bother him all the time because he is famous and he played fucking RYAN. However, I figure if Amy Schumer asks if she can take the photo, he will be okay with it. I tell Amy that I need to borrow her famousness and she is immediately on board. We walk over.

The woman he is with, on closer inspection, turns out to be Morena Baccarin, the gorgeous doe-eyed angel who played Brody's wife on *Homeland*. I have never seen a woman less troubled by another woman approaching her boyfriend than Morena Baccarin was by me going up to Ben McKenzie.

I tap him on the shoulder and say "Hi" and then Amy jumps in and says she wants to take a picture of us. He looks at us quizzically but smiles (my heart stops) and says "Sure" and then he puts his arm around me.[3] Just as Amy is about to take the picture, he turns toward me with a slightly worried look on his face and says:

"Hold on, wait. Is this some kind of in-joke between you guys?"

---

3   If you are curious what it feels like to have Ben McKenzie's arm around you, it's like being in the womb. You feel like you are asleep under a cashmere rainbow. You feel safe. You feel like nothing bad could ever happen to you again.

I study his face. He is serious. He's genuinely concerned that our interest in taking this photo is ironic. That we are somehow making fun of him.

And that is when it dawns on me:

Even Ben McKenzie feels a little bit like dogshit.

But how could this be possible? He was the star of *The O.C.*! He was Ryan! He is also on some show now called *Gotham* that I have never watched but I am sure is wonderful because he is in it. And yet, as he chats with his girlfriend, beauteous Brazilian gift-from-above MORENA BACCARIN, in the VIP EMMY LOUNGE, he is insecure enough about his stature that he's worried he's the butt of a joke. That maybe he is being compared to his former *O.C.* self and found lacking.

Even Ben McKenzie does not feel like a Prinzezzz.

Ben McKenzie, who has everything.

Years ago, I read an interview with Nicole Kidman where she talked about winning her Oscar for *The Hours*. At the same time that she was at the peak moment of her career, arguably of anyone's career, she was also going through her divorce from Tom Cruise. She said that after she won, she found herself back at her hotel room early, by herself, feeling as alone and sad as she'd ever felt in her life. I remember liking Nicole Kidman very much for revealing that information, but also not totally believing her. Surely, I thought, even when Nicole Kidman is sad, she can't ever be that sad. And of course it is a cliché that the very rich and very beautiful and very famous can be miserable, and Marilyn Monroe committed suicide, and Owen Wilson tried to commit suicide, and we are all human. But it was hard for me to imagine having those feelings while holding that golden statue. Surely there must be some protective magic in it, at least for a little while.

So how surprising to find myself having won an Emmy, in the basement of the Nokia Theatre, topless and alone. I am breast-pumping in a little bare dressing room. My friends have gone on to the post-ceremony dinner and I've told them I'll join them there. With the pump making its *wuhm mmm wuhm mmm wuhm mmm* noise, I watch my nipples pulled outward and then back. My once cute little pink nipples, now turned into odd brown inchworms. My postpartum stomach has gotten fat the way indoor cats' stomachs get fat, with a large wavy flap of skin that droops low over the elastic of my Spanx, and would get in the way if I tried to jump to the top of a refrigerator.

My Emmy is on the floor. I am not the loneliest I've ever felt, but I am not the happiest, either. *This is what it feels like to be here*, I think, but strangely enough I cannot tell exactly what I am feeling. I try to figure out if this is enough. I have a baby. I have a husband. I have an Emmy. These seem like things everyone wants. But then there are the buts. But I am scared of the future. But I don't know what my next job will be. But I am surrounded by people more famous and more rich than me. But I don't believe in myself. But what if I never get past the point of helping other, more confident people achieve their dreams. But I am a footnote to others' success. But I am on Zoloft because of a deep depression that set in while I was pregnant (it's helping).

I feel like I'm not really here, even though I'm here. It's the same feeling I had when I started working on *SNL* and I went to the afterparty for the first time—the legendarily coolest party in NYC. I expected to feel the relief of finally being in. But as I was ushered to a table in the immediate front with the other new writers and interns, I realized that the real party was in the back. And in the back, the real party was at Lorne's table. And even at Lorne's table, the real party is probably only in Lorne's head. And in Lorne's head, Lorne is the only person allowed in. I think maybe Paul Simon is also there.

Much is made of the modern phenomenon of FOMO—the fear of missing out—spawned by millions of Instagram and Facebook and Twitter photos of people having more fun than you, being closer to the ocean than you, showing off better tits and ass than you, standing closer to celebrities than you. You think, *I wish I was there, not here.* But then you get there. And you think, *I thought here would be different. I thought it would be more like there. But it's more like here again.* And it never ends.

I would keep pondering this, but I am finished pumping. I pull my dress back on, struggling to zip the back on my own, and walk into the bathroom, where I pour my breast milk into the sink and watch the white go down the drain.

Get the Epidural

Mike and I are sitting in a circle with eight other pregnant couples. Our childbirth education leader, Carol, has just asked if we would like to see what a contraction might look like. Like Bartleby, I would really prefer not to. Everyone else, however, nods yes, they would very much like to see a contraction. Carol sits back in her chair and closes her eyes. She makes a low "mmmm" noise that stops and then starts again louder. To my horror, Carol begins to moan, and gradually slumps off her chair until she is on the floor on all fours, groaning and hitting the ground with her fist. I feel many things watching this. I am embarrassed. I want to leave. I am already terrified of birth, but now I am also terrified of Carol. Her moans eventually get lower until they cease, and she returns to her chair, quiet, eyes closed for another few moments before she opens them again and gets out of "character."

"What did you think?" she asks the group.

One woman says she's interested in learning positions

to help with the pain. Another woman says she's afraid but excited to give birth. A woman who seems like she might be a little bit of an asshole raises her hand. She turns out to be me.

"I think, I don't want to do that," I blurt out. I tell everyone I am seriously considering an elective C-section, because I am. Everyone looks at me like I just said I am seriously considering throwing a puppy off a roof.

For the rest of the class, Carol leads the group in a slow, meandering discussion of pain management methods that allow you to avoid an epidural. To my amazement, none of my fellow preggos seem to want one. They talk about getting an epidural as if they are talking about getting gonorrhea. There are some hedges about maybe getting a "walking" epidural or a "late and light" epidural. My head is exploding.

Carol says she's going to show us a video of women in labor. "It's not scary, I promise," she says. She pops in a DVD and then, not surprisingly, struggles with the AV for a few minutes. Finally, she gets it to play, and we are seeing a hospital in what appears to be the late 1970s, based on the porn mustaches of the dads and the curly 'fros of the moms (both black and white). We watch the women in hospital gowns walking up and down the halls, supported by their partners, sweating and staggering. One woman is in her labor room, holding on to a bar on the wall and whispering to herself like she is possessed. Another is in the hospital bed, eyes closed, a grimace on her face. There's fifteen minutes of this stuff, and then we cut to some of the actual births. I've always avoided watching birth videos. But now I'm being forced to watch this, like I'm in *A Clockwork Orange*, and I can't look away. We see one baby come shooting out of a vagina, purple as a plum, and for the first time in my life I see what the umbilical cord really looks like. It's blue and looks like fifty Twizzlers twisted together.

Carol snaps off the TV. "See?" she says, grinning. "None of those women had epidurals. And they looked okay, right?"

I do not think they looked okay.

Five hours later, we are wrapping up. There is still another whole day of this tomorrow. This is a two-day intensive class for which we have paid hundreds of dollars. Carol asks if anyone has any final questions. An Italian woman with a cute accent raises her hand.

"Erm, I am just curious, um, just, why does everyone not want an epidural? I do not want it, either, I am just curious as to why others don't."

Carol's brow furrowed. Everyone's brow furrowed. Except mine. My brow didn't furrow. I don't know what the opposite of furrow is. Let's just say it unfurrowed.

It unfurrowed because if there is one thing I want you to get out of this book, and I am not putting any pressure on you to get anything out of it, but if I were to tell you one thing that I would want you to close the covers of this book and walk away convinced of, it would be this:

GET THE EPIDURAL.

GET THE EPIDURAL.

When you write an email and you use all-caps, people don't like it because they say it seems like you're screaming. They're right. I am screaming.

GET THE EPIDURAL.

I mean, if you really want to give birth without medication, and it is important to you, and you are absolutely certain that you are the only one telling yourself that you want to birth your baby this way, then by all means, go ahead. But if you are Googling around and feeling unsure, or your mother-in-law is telling you that she did it without the epidural (she doesn't remember correctly, I assure you), or some doula is pressuring you to give birth at home in a tub filled with quinoa, basically, if you have a shadow of a doubt…

GET THE EPIDURAL.

Not only do I recommend getting an epidural while you're giving birth, I'd say get one beforehand. I'm sitting here writing, and I would get an epidural right now if I could.

I have gone online to try to understand what reasoning there is for women not to get an epidural. The top reasons seem to be:

1. You can't feel yourself pushing.
2. You're numb and can't move.
3. There's an increased risk of C-section.

I will now quickly address these assertions. (Let me add now that I know every woman is different, and every labor is different, and we are all snowflakes, and I am definitely not a doctor, but on the other hand...GET THE EPIDURAL.)

1. **Re: You can't feel yourself pushing.**

So, I had an epidural. And not just any epidural. I demanded it as soon as I got to the hospital and I told them to turn it all the way up until the knob might come off. Hours later, when I was fully dilated (ew) and it was time to push, I experienced an intense need to poop. If you want to know what it felt like, I can't describe it in any other way except it felt like I was going to give birth to an armadillo out of my butthole. When you get this sensation, your entire body wants to help this armadillo escape and is willing to assist by any means necessary. Not only will you push, but you will push with every molecule in your body. I pushed, and I felt myself pushing. That said, I would have loved to feel absolutely nothing. I would have loved to give birth the way women did in the 1950s when they were basically chloroformed with a rag at eight months pregnant and didn't wake up till their baby was two weeks old. I don't know why we stopped doing this.

2. **Re: You're numb and can't move.**

This was not true for me. I could feel my legs and move my legs, though I probably could not have stood if I wanted to. That said, I didn't really want to move. Once I got my epidural, I lay still on the hospital bed staring at the wall-mounted TV, happily watching an epic marathon of *Sex and the City* on mute. I had it on mute because I know every line of dialogue in every episode of that show, and also I was enjoying the peaceful beeps and blips coming from my fetal monitor, after a shitshow of a morning that included vomiting from the pain of my contractions. Also, I was entitled to unlimited ice pops, the kind I ate as a kid that come in long plastic tubes that you have to bite your way through. I did this for six hours. How often in this life do you get to lie in bed eating ice pops and watching *Sex and the City* for six hours? Please continue reading to reason #3...

3. Re: There's an increased risk of C-section.

I suppose you could argue that if your labor wasn't progressing, and a new position would have helped but you can't get into that position because you have an epidural, you might end up needing an emergency C-section. But what would that lead to? Probably recovering in bed, getting to watch more *Sex and the City* and eating more ice pops.

This seems like a classic win-win.

GET THE EPIDURAL.

Why do so many women feel like they shouldn't get an epidural?

Consider this.

I am seven months pregnant and standing on line at a grocery in Brooklyn, minding my own business (as much as anyone pregnant can mind their own business, because people constantly feel like they have the right to talk to pregnant women about their pregnancy). A woman in front of me turns around. She's a little younger than me. She does not appear pregnant. She is not with kids. Maybe she has kids at home. It doesn't really matter.

She asks me, "When are you due?"

This is a common question and one I don't mind answering, although I have never felt compelled to ask anything of a pregnant woman that I don't know.

I say, "June twenty-seventh." I assume we are done.

But then, she says:

"Are you having a natural birth?"

I'm just trying to buy a sandwich. Is this complete stranger really asking about my plans re: my vagina? I cannot believe this. Still, I decide to be honest.

"Fuck no," I reply with a smile.

She looks at me, worried. "So…you're having an epidural?"

I am beside myself. "Why don't you go fuck yourself," I tell her.

(Okay, I didn't say that. Instead I said:)

"Yes. At the very *least*."

Now she looks genuinely shocked. She turns and scurries away, like a missionary who's just been told by a particularly stubborn native that she's very excited to go directly to Pagan Hell.

I have thought about this conversation often. It annoyed me the rest of that day, and many days after, and recalling it now, I'm annoyed again. I just had to eat a cookie to stop being annoyed. But at the center of this interaction is one of the key little acorns of bullshit that perpetuates this guilt over epidurals.

The term *natural birth.*

"Natural." It sounds so…natural. So relaxing. So earth goddess. So feminine.

But how often do people really want women to be or do anything "natural"?

It seems to me the answer is almost never. In fact, almost everything "natural" about women is considered pretty fucking horrific. Hairy legs and armpits? Please shave, you furry beast. And while you're at it, don't forget to remove your pubic hair, that's also an abomination. Do you have hips and cellulite? Please go hide in the very back of your shoe closet and turn the light off and stay there until someone tells you to come out (no one will tell you to come out).

It's interesting that no one cares very much about women doing anything "naturally" until it involves them being in excruciating pain.

No one ever asks a man if he's having a "natural root canal." No one ever asks if a man is having a "natural vasectomy."

GET THE EPIDURAL.

"But what about the science," some women (and many men) will say. "There is science supporting all the estimated 'risks' of an epidural!" Well, again, I am not a doctor, but I do have the Internet. And I've Googled the pros and cons extensively, which is very close to what a doctor would do. And the fact is there's science supporting both sides. There's a boatload of science that says having an epidural is totally fine. And for everyone arguing that epidurals slow your labor down, there are all the doctors who say that epidurals actually speed your labor up.

There are so many debates in this life in which there is some evidence of one thing, and also some evidence of the other. At such a point, you just have to decide what to believe. So here's a radical idea: Why not believe the thing that makes you happy? Why not disavow the argument that means you will be writhing in pain for umpteen hours and just GET THE EPIDURAL. You probably already see the wisdom of this philosophy in other areas of your life. For example: There is that old rumor that Richard Gere once had to go to the emergency room because there was a hamster stuck up his butt. I can either believe this, or not believe it. It's way more fun to believe it, so I do.

GET THE EPIDURAL.

And finally, I offer you this thought.

Shortly before my son was born, I spoke to a friend on the phone about how guilty I felt that we were planning to hire a night nurse for a few weeks. Shouldn't I be the one to take care of him all the time? He was my peanut that I had created. Wouldn't I be shirking my maternal responsibilities if I didn't stay up around the clock? I was worried that I was already a failure.

At which point my friend said, "What are you trying to win?"

What was I trying to win? I thought about it and realized—nothing. There's nothing to win.

There is so much pressure on women around birth and labor and mothering to do it one way or another. It's so easy to believe the notion that having a baby demands complete and total sacrifice, and anything short of that is not enough. That if you're not in pain, you're selfish.

But here's the thing: If you're worried that skipping the pain of childbirth means you're somehow cheating your baby, or yourself, you're not. Because the truth is, life offers more than enough pain that you will not be able to skip. By the time you've had a kid, you've probably been through some of it already. The pain of breakups. The pain of rejection. The pain of being picked last for a team. The pain of hearing your parents fighting in the other room. When you have a baby, there will be plenty more pain. The pain of recovery, no matter how you give birth. The pain of nursing. The pain of not fitting into any of your old clothes. The pain of not even fitting into your maternity jeans. The pain of hearing your baby cry and not knowing how to fix it. The pain of wondering whether your partner still finds you attractive. The pain of arguing with your husband while your child is in the other room.

The pain of knowing that you witnessed the very first moment of this beautiful person's life, and that one day, hopefully at least a hundred years from now, there will inevitably be a last moment.

So really…

Get the epidural.

The Infertility Chapters

1. TRYING

I have always hated the phrase *We're trying*, which couples generally use to describe their attempts at conceiving a child. I used to think it was because of the slightly prissy euphemistic quality of it, the substitution of the wan *trying* for *fucking*; but when I thought harder about it, I realized maybe it's because *trying* evokes so much struggle; in a way, it's the opposite of a euphemism. Maybe it's all too accurate, and what I don't like about it is how graphically it paints a portrait of two people joylessly having intercourse in an attempt to breed.

Trying.

I'd made up my mind long ago that I would never be one of those ladies who was *trying*. It sounded so sad and desperate, and I wasn't sad and desperate. I'd never wanted a baby. In my mid-thirties, I thought this primal urge might kick in, but it didn't, and I was glad it didn't, because then I would become someone who talked about trying. Or even worse, blogged about it.

By my late thirties, I still didn't want a baby. At most, as forty approached and became an increasingly realer number that was probably going to happen to me at some point in the terrifyingly near future, I had a dim feeling that it might be nice to have a kid when I was old. More specifically, I would think about being on my deathbed (I'm fun), and how if there was no kid, it would be sad and lonely (for me—I didn't think about how the kid would feel).

So basically, when I imagined having a kid, I projected forty years into the future, in which I visualized a fully grown adult spoon-feeding me pudding on my way out of this earthly door. I wasn't worried about feeling a kid void before this life moment.

Then I got married.

Before we got engaged, Mike and I had a few vague, hypothetical conversations about whether we would have a kid. I very clearly remember that in all of these conversations, we were both on the same page, which is to say we agreed we were completely ambivalent. Then, about a month after our wedding, it came up again, and magically, Mike had a different memory of our conversations. Somehow, he remembered us both saying we would definitely have kids. As you might imagine, this led to a rather large fight, in which I tried to remind him that our favorite activities were going to restaurants and drinking, two things that most certainly would be curtailed by the presence of a child. I challenged his recall of how I'd phrased my interest in us having a baby. I'd always said I loved our life, that it was hard for me to picture the disruption of our rambling routines. He ended up storming out of the house and I retreated to our bedroom to look at pictures of corgis on Pinterest.

I knew it was inevitable, with Mike feeling so strongly about it, that we were going to have a kid. But we'd just gotten married. I didn't want to try yet. I was thirty-eight. I thought I probably had some time left. Halle Berry had just gotten pregnant again and she was like a million years old. I was scared of how everything would change once we had a kid. I thought maybe we could at least wait till the summer. I kept thinking to myself, *This is the last year of my life.* I repeated that phrase in my head—*last year of my life, last year of my life.* I better enjoy it, it's the last real year of my life. And I would say to Mike, This could all be moot you know, maybe I'm already too old, maybe I'm *barren.* Barren is a fun word to toss around with your husband when you're being a real fucking jerk. But I was just making excuses; I knew I wasn't barren, because my mom had three kids, and she had my little sister when she was thirty-six, which is basically the same as thirty-eight.

Still, the next time I went to see my ob-gyn, I figured it wouldn't be a bad idea to ask her, in her professional opinion, how long I had to wait before I had a kid (instantly, with no trying). Again, I wasn't worried because at that moment Halle Berry was expecting and she's sixty-four I think? I knew I wouldn't be able to wait quite that long but I thought maybe I could wait as long as some other celebrities I'd read about in my trash magazines.

A quick word about my doctor, Dr. Sani. She's incredibly hip. I know she must be older than me, but she looks about five years younger. She grew up in New York, went to the same high school as me, and used to do a little deejaying in college. She's compassionate, she never rushes you, and she's delightfully down to earth. She's also gorgeous. This can be a problem since I always miss a small portion of her advice while I am entranced by her curtain of perfectly shiny thick black hair.

At the appointment we spent the usual time gabbing about my job and the weather and vacations, and I stared at her hair a bit. When we got up to babies, as expected, she didn't seem overly concerned. "Most thirty-eight-year-olds can get pregnant without too much trouble. The problem is usually more with staying pregnant." I ignored the second sentence.

It was December at the time. She thought if I wanted I could wait till the end of the following year. That felt like enough time to live the last year of my life. She went on to suggest that if we wanted some peace of mind, I could do a relatively new but simple blood test that would measure a hormone called AMH. She explained that it measured the quality of your egg reserve, or maybe it was the quantity, I was never totally sure (again, staring at her hair). We'd done other blood tests and she felt optimistic I was in good health and had nothing to worry about. She left the room and the nurse came in to take my blood and I went home and stopped thinking about babies entirely. I had the slightly smug feeling you have when you know you will be fine because you've always been fine.

A couple of weeks later, she called to tell me that I needed to redo the test. "The number that came back didn't really make any sense," she said, "and then I found out that they didn't freeze your sample in transit. Let's not worry about it. I'm sure it's fine, just redo it." For about sixty seconds after we got off the phone, I replayed the sound of her voice, trying to discern if she was genuinely unconcerned or was hiding something. I used the same filter I use when I'm flying and I need to look at a flight attendant to assess whether turbulence is going to kill me or not. I decided to believe her.

A few days later, I go to a lab to have my blood taken again. I make calm casual conversation with the woman who will be taking my blood so she will know I'm not a puss about having my blood drawn (I'm a giant puss about having blood drawn). I walk out of there feeling very confident that this version of the test will confirm that I am totally healthy and can probably wait as long as, if not Halle Berry, then maybe Salma Hayek (first child at forty-one).

A couple of weeks later, I am at an edit facility, watching cuts of the show I write for. It is near the end of the day. My phone rings. It is my doctor. This time, even though she is, as always, professional and calm, her voice does not completely pass the flight attendant test; at best the cabin is out of white wine. At worst an engine is sputtering.

"Your numbers did not come back exactly where we'd want them to be," she began to explain.

My cell reception was not good and I did not have privacy. I kept moving from one dark exit stairwell to another, trying to hear her as she explained, in so many words, that I would become a woman who would not only have to try, but would have to try very, very hard. She had wanted my number to be at least a 2. Instead, my number came back as <.16, which is the lowest the test can measure before your ovaries are emitting a life signal so weak it can no longer be quantified.

As she spoke, for the first time in my life, I felt as if a ghost were passing through me; that someone else, some infertile, trying and failing sad person, had mistakenly crossed their fate with mine. *This can't be my life*, I kept thinking, even though it now most definitely was.

And the other thing I suddenly couldn't stop thinking was, *I want a baby*.

2. DR. BANDER

Dr. Sani recommends a fertility practice. She says there are several doctors there who are all very good, but the one whose name she remembers off the top of her head is a Dr. Bander. Sani says she will call her and tell her about me.

I make an appointment with Dr. Bander. I go to the practice's website and look at pictures of her. I like to know what my doctors are going to look like before I go to them. She looks pretty in her photo. I notice that she, too, has very beautiful hair that is styled into a sweeping shoulder-length coif, like the kind you see on home hair dye boxes.

When Mike and I arrive at her office on the Upper East Side, I see the walls are covered with "Best Doctor" awards and accolades. This is comforting until I look closely and realize they are for the two other doctors who work with the one I am seeing.

The waiting room is small, but lots of women, with husbands and boyfriends and partners in tow, are coming in and out with some frequency. I have the same unsettling feeling I used to get when I would occasionally go to auditions and would notice that all the other girls and I were vague facsimiles of each other. In that situation, it was amusingly depressing. Here, even though the women around me are of all shapes, sizes, and colors, our common thread is just regular depressing. I don't want to be here. I don't want to be with all these women who are *trying*.

Dr. Bander calls us into her office. We've been sitting for two seconds when she begins our appointment my least favorite way doctors begin appointments:

"How can I help you?"

This always feels so abrupt. I'd prefer we start with some small talk so we can get to know each other. Maybe one of us could make a little joke. And it seems silly to ask "How can I help you" when you are a fertility doctor. No der, we want to have a fucking baby.

"I think my doctor, Sani, told you about me?" I say.

She is blank. "Um…maybe…how can I help you?"

This is already not going super great. Apparently she did not get the memo that I am very special and should be treated accordingly.

I explain that even though we have not yet started *trying*, I have received a bummer number on a blood test. I assume she will give us a cheerful overview of the trying process. Because we don't know anything. Instead, she starts detailing all the tests I will need to have, all the drugs I should start taking, and all the drugs I will most likely have to take after the initial drugs fail. I will apparently have to come in every week for blood tests for "monitoring," although she does not make clear to me what I will be monitored for. She also tells me that a week after my next period I have to schedule a test called a hysnerfohysteragram (not what it's actually called, but what it sounds like in that moment). She puts a sonogram picture of a uterus on a light box on her wall and explains that this test is to see if one of my fallopian tubes is blocked. I recognize the basic female reproductive system diagram that my high school bio teacher drew on the board, the one that looked like a longhorn cow's head.

"How do you do that test?" I ask.

No big deal, she explains. A catheter is just inserted

through your cervix and then a dye—or something like a dye? maybe Diet Coke—is slowly pumped into your uterus and if it flows into your tubes, you're fine. If one or both tubes don't show the dye, that means there's a clog and maybe they have to put Drano in it or something?

She hands me one of those blurry, over-Xeroxed pieces of paper that often go along with medical tests, listing the instructions. No eating for four hours before, but I am to take six hundred milligrams of Motrin to "reduce cramping."

"Is the test really painful?" I ask Bander.

"It's not bad if you take the Motrin," she says, shuffling other papers on her desk.

I already know this test is going to be horrendous. I have never liked instruments poking around my cervix. The very idea of my cervix, or any cervix, fills me with dread. There's something about the existence of this very tiny hole at the back of my vagina that leads to my insides that makes me shudder. I don't like the idea of anything going IN there, which I realize makes no sense seeing as I am doing all this to get something rather enormous to come out of there.

Dr. Bander writes me a prescription for some hormone pill and tells me that once I've taken it for five days I will come in for an injection that will make me ovulate. Then it will be time to have sex.

"And you don't have to have sex every day. Every other day is fine," she says.

"But it should be vaginal, right?" I say.

No one laughs at my hilarious joke.

For the next three months, I take a forty-five-minute subway ride from Brooklyn to the Upper East Side to get my weekly blood test. I have to confess to a variety of nurses that I have a tendency to faint when dealing with needles. I tell them I have to look away, and they have to make small talk with me while I'm being pricked. No one enjoys this. I'm desperate for the nurses to like me, so I always pick something about their appearance to compliment—their clothes or hair or jewelry. I know it's not necessary and even I don't like that I do it, but I can't stop.

When they finish drawing my blood, they put a little balled-up piece of gauze on the prick and tell me to hold it while they open a Band-Aid. The Band-Aid goes over the gauze but the gauze always spills out from under it a bit, like a marshmallow oozing out from a s'more. Then I walk to the front desk and give my credit card to one of the grumpy ladies at the desk, who charges $200 to my credit card. As I sign the slip, I think about all the other things I would have loved to spend $200 on.

I walk two blocks back to the subway and ride another forty-five minutes back home. A few hours later, a nurse calls to tell me what my estrogen and progesterone levels are. These numbers are always meaningless to me.

Dr. Bander has also told me to buy an over-the-counter supplement called DHEA, which is supposed to boost ovarian function. I go to the pharmacy and buy the bottle. When I get home I read the label and discover that the side effects are acne and hair loss. I stand in the bathroom and ponder whether I'm ready for acne and hair loss. I decide I'm not and throw the bottle, unopened, under the sink. To make up for it, I pop the baby aspirin that Dr. Bander also told me to take every day. That seems easier.

Four weeks later, I get severe tinnitus in my left ear, which apparently can happen with consistent aspirin use. Or so the ear specialist informed me as he let me know that tinnitus is almost impossible to cure and usually stays with you for life. My tinnitus is like the sound of static on a bad phone line connection, a dull tone that goes up and down.

This is trying.

3. SOTI (STAY OFF THE INTERNET, AND OTHER ACRONYMS)

One of the things that happens when you find out you might be infertile is you suddenly have an intense drive to use the Internet as a Magic 8 Ball. You shake it over and over, entering your exact hormone numbers into your Google toolbar to see if any other trying person with the same numbers has had any luck having a baby. It's a truly stupid thing to do, and yet you do it anyway. I started Googling "amh less than .16" and immediately found myself sliding down a rabbit hole of infertility websites, chat rooms, and forums. All of them are haunted by a dreary sadness. And that's saying something, considering the sad horror that is most of the Internet. "Trying" always feels acutely sad on these forums because if you're on one of those sites it means you're currently "Failing."

Still (and this is going to be controversial), I can't help but think the other ladies on these sites could stand to lighten up just the tiniest smidge. I feel guilty for feeling this way but also I can't help it. While I sometimes plumb the depths of this animal, irrational sadness at not being able to get pregnant, I also want to be able to laugh, just occasionally, at the absurdity of what we are putting ourselves through.

The other thing about these sites is they are written in their own special language, one made up almost entirely of acronyms and numbers. The very few words that aren't acronyms are emojis. It looks like some kind of code that might be used in a war, and actually, it is. All of these women are at war with their own bodies, these bodies that are stubbornly not giving them what they want.

Entering these forums can feel like you've accidentally walked through a door at the back of your closet leading into a very bleak Narnia. As soon as I began exploring them, I had a strong, visceral instinct to quickly and quietly exit while closing the door forever. That is what I should have done. And ultimately, it's what I did. However: In the mania that is trying, I wanted to decode the code, because perhaps somewhere, in someone else's story, I might find a happy ending to my story. Unfortunately, infertility forums are not chockablock with happy endings. There are a million long Russian novels about ovaries and IVFs and miscarriages, oh my. Many posters' online signatures read like histories of their entire genome. For instance, someone named Lisa might sign off with:

TTC since 11-12. PCOS, DH LSC. 3 IUI with Clomid all BFN. FTTA

After Googling, I found out those letters meant:

TTC—trying to conceive
PCOS—polycystic ovary syndrome
DH—dear husband
LSC—low sperm count
IUI—intrauterine insemination
BFN—big fat negative (i.e., pregnancy test)
FTTA—fertile thoughts to all

At first I found the reliance on acronyms annoying—was it necessary for these women to abbreviate every single little thing? And eventually I realized it was, because they are spending so much of their time on trying to get pregnant, with the doctors and the shots and the acupuncture and the yoga, that there is literally not enough time to spell words out in their entirety.

Here are some infertility acronyms I came up with:

HAS—home alone, spiraling
FO—freaking out
STBOOTBOA—scared to become one of those
baby-obsessed assholes
GDAOTI—getting drunk and on the Internet
INMFIDGME—it's not my fault I didn't get
married earlier
HPOUMBAETRNWDID—had planned on using
my baby as excuse to retire, now what do I do?
NESWTAMBUIA—not even sure what this
acronym means but using it anyway
VD—very drunk

4. THE HSG

It is finally time for my hysterosnuffleupagusgram. I'm
nervous but I've taken my Motrin and I've arranged to
meet a girlfriend after the test just to celebrate that it's
over. I keep telling myself that I'm a grown-up and
grown-ups have to take tests and just be grown-up about
it. But I still have that nervous shaky feeling that dogs get
when they hop in the car to go to the vet. They *know* they
ain't going to the park.

I'm meeting Dr. Bander at a hospital, where she will
perform the test. I sit in the waiting room of the gynecological ultrasound room. I watch the women walking
out and try to gauge how much pain they seem to be in.

All of them seem fine. No limping. No one is bleeding out. Then my name is called and a nurse leads me to one of those sad little changing rooms where you take everything off and put on a paper gown and inevitably get a little lost wandering to where you're supposed to go and have to cover your exposed butt with your hands.

I make it to the room and try not to look at the tubing and tools that will soon be going into my cervix. Ew, my cervix! Dr. Bander shows me the screen we will watch to see if my fallopian tubes (ew again) are open enough to fill with the dye. The part that can cause cramping, Dr. Bander explains as she clamps open my vagina with the ice cream scoopy thingy,[1] is when she uses a catheter to push the fluid dye into the cervix. The pressure of the dye itself is technically supposed to be the problem. However, as soon as she starts to insert the catheter, I feel an intense pain and let out a yelp.

"I'm barely even touching you," Dr. Bander says tersely. I'm not sure why she is telling me this. She makes another attempt with the catheter and again I let out a yelp.

"You have a very sensitive cervix," she informs me. She seems annoyed with me, which is a bit of a mystery since I am the one who is stuck with the crappy cervix. "I'm going to try to use a different instrument."

She uses the different tool that hurts slightly less,

---

1   Speculum.

which begs the question of why she wouldn't have used the less painful tool in the first place. Then she begins to fill my insides with the dye fluid[2] and I experience a whole other level of pain. It feels like someone is punching me in the stomach over and over. I flinch and Bander tells me not to move as I start profusely sweating.

A few minutes later we are done. She presses PLAYBACK on the monitor to show me as one fallopian tube, thin as a hair, goes dark with the fluid. On the other side, there is nothing. "Well," she says matter-of-factly, "your left tube is totally open and clear. The right tube did not fill. So either it's blocked, or else your cramping was just so severe that it temporarily blocked the tube."

Can I get pregnant with one blocked tube?

Technically yes, she says. But it's harder.

I ask her what the upshot is.

"It's inconclusive," she says. "But really, your reaction to the test was unusually difficult. When you have a baby, you'll definitely need to get an epidural."

When you have a baby.

If we are so sure it is "when" and not "if," why did we just inflate my innards like a water balloon?

And no doy! Of course I'm getting an epidural, you monster.

She leaves. I am led back to the sad little changing room where I am given a plump hot dog bun of a maxi pad to

---

2   The Diet Coke.

contain my post-test bleeding. My stomach is still cramping. I limp the three blocks to Magnolia Bakery, where my friend Zubeida is meeting me for a pint of banana pudding. Banana pudding has been my go-to feel-sorry-for-myself treat for many years. Usually I eat it after breakups and Mets losses. Now I'm eating it because one of my fallopian tubes is apparently garbage and also my cervix is a disaster. I finish an entire pudding pint, only to realize my feelings are still stubbornly feelable, thus necessitating an extra red velvet cupcake to try to stuff them back into the sand. I definitely do not enjoy the cupcake and 100 percent feel worse when it has been deposited on top of the feeling pile. Now I'm barren AND fat, I whine to myself.

On the subway ride home, I luxuriate in a hot tub of self-pity. I think of a new acronym:

IABFDB—I'm a barren fat dumb bitch

A few weeks after the test, Dr. Bander tells me that if I'm not pregnant by August, I should definitely plan on doing IVF because I am running out of time. She wants me to start doing shots. I hate needles, and the idea of having to learn to administer them at home myself necessitates more pudding, cupcakes, and ice cream. As someone who primarily writes sex jokes for a living, this task seems beyond my ken. My husband supposedly could learn to do it, but he has sausage fingers and by his own admission is terrible at small, detailed tasks requiring dexterity. If he cannot help me zip up a dress, I do not feel great about him plunging a syringe into my body. I ask her about trying an IUI[3] before moving on to IVF (acronyms!) and she tells me it's a waste of time.

I fire Dr. Bander.

5. DR. MUKHERJEE

My beloved primary care doctor, Dr. Rahman, recommends Dr. Mukherjee as my new fertility Sherpa. We show up to his office on a warm afternoon in May, and I like him immediately. He grew up in the Bronx and has the build and bearing of John Madden, if John Madden were Indian and fiddled with ladies' baby junk for a living.

Even his office has a different vibe. He is a part of a very large practice, and it's constantly packed with the women who make up our strange club—Hasidic women, black women, white women, young women, older women, and very rich women bedecked in very fancy jewelry, which for all its fanciness still has not bought them a baby. The sound system is always playing upbeat contemporary pop, which I suppose is better than depressing music—I mean, who wants to contemplate their barrenness to Portishead or Pink Floyd?—but on the

---

3 Intrauterine insemination. In layman's terms, your husband/boyfriend/donor spooges into a jar and then the contents of that jar are gooshed up your puss with a turkey baster. SCIENCE!

other hand it's no less surreal to wait for your estrogen levels to be measured for the umpteenth time to Whitney Houston's "Million Dollar Bill."

Unlike Dr. Bander, who treated the fertility process with the cold exacting manner of a scientist herding lab rats, Dr. Mukherjee's attitude resembles more closely that of a high school football coach who truly believes the game isn't about winning or losing but should really be about Fun! I like this attitude.

I ask him if he thinks I need to be rushing into IVF.

"Nah, you just started trying," he says with a wave of the hand. "Let's give you a chance, see how it goes."

I pepper him with more questions, making up a few to hide the one that is most important, which is obviously how much I can drink while the Trying process is happening.

"Don't get blackout drunk," he says. "But beyond that you're fine."

This is tremendous news. I consider leaving Mike to marry Dr. Mukherjee.

We agree that for the next three months I will take a pill that will help me sprout extra follicles (ew, follicles!) in the middle of my cycle (ew, cycle!). I will come to the office for an ultrasound wherein we will count follicles, and if there are enough (but also not too many), I will receive an injection of Ovidrel into my stomach, which will induce my eggs (barf, eggs!) to slide down my tubes (no words). At which point Mike and I will know it is time to bang it out for a few days. "Doesn't have to be every day, every other day is fine," Mukherjee says. I decide to quit while we're all ahead and not to do my vaginal/anal joke even though I feel like Mukherjee would totally get it.

As we are wrapping up, he says there is one other thing we should do before we begin this phase of Trying. "Have you done your HSG yet?" he asks.

"You should have the results," I say with the eager smugness of a teacher's pet who did all the homework before being asked.

He shuffles through my incredibly thick file.

"Hm."

?

"You should redo the test," he says. "You wanna know what's up with that other tube."

I ask if it's really necessary because, not to be all dramatic, but the last test was the worst thing that's ever happened to me.[4]

"Yeah, well," he says as he eats half a meatball sandwich (he wasn't really eating a meatball sandwich, but that is always his vibe). "You don't want to waste your time trying to get pregnant with just one tube if you could have both tubes. If you only have one tube open we should try to do something about it."

Do something about it?

"Yeah, the doctor I'm gonna send you to could blow it open if it's blocked."

---

4   Me = my uterus.

Blow it open?

He explains that a blocked tube can literally have air blown into it to try to clear it out. This brings the plumbing analogy to new heights. Or rather, depths.

6. THE HSG PART 2—DR. BRADY

I show up for my second hysterosnuffleupagus. I have been told that for this test I will be sedated, which is heartening, but then I inquire further and discover that I will not be completely unconscious, as I'd been hoping. Anything short of complete blackness feels like not enough.

Dr. Brady's practice is one of those Upper East Side shmancy offices where there is a doorman who lets you in and dark wood everywhere and nice carpeting that you would maybe even choose to have in your house. However, these amenities fade into the background as my appointment, for which I have been instructed not to eat or drink eight hours prior, gets pushed farther and farther into the day. I arrive at nine a.m.; by noon I am starving and my nerves are frayed. I've instructed Mike to pick me up with banana pudding in hand.

At one, I am finally led to the sad little paper gown room. I am then guided to a dimly lit surgical suite where I lie on a steel table. I'm so scared I'm physically shaking. The nurses begin prepping my arm for the sedation IV as the doctor comes in.

"What are you giving me?" I ask. He tells me it's a

mixture of morphine and Demerol. I ask if they can maybe crank it up a smooch so I'm knocked out. He says they need me to be awake so I can respond and move during the test. I explain that I have a very special cervix that's particularly sensitive and thus I should get double the normal amount of drugs, and as I am making my case, the drugs enter my vein and in about two seconds I am enveloped by a wave of joy. It gently smooths out all the anxiety and fear and depression I have been feeling about this test, and Trying in general. It's unlike anything I've ever experienced, this sudden rush of relief from everything in my life that doesn't feel like warm velvet.

The high also makes me completely silly, even though I'm not aware of it.

"Tilt your pelvis a little to the left," Dr. Brady says.

"Do you guys smoke pot?" I ask him and the nurses. "We should all smoke pot together."

They don't respond. I realize maybe there's been a misunderstanding.

"I don't mean now. Right now you guys are doing a procedure on me. But later. Another time."

There is still no response. I think to myself, *I can't believe I'm bombing my own procedure.* It turns out I'm actually saying it, not thinking it.

"And tilt to the other side," Dr. Brady says.

I tilt. Wheeee!

This is what heroin must feel like, I think. *Maybe I should do heroin.*

"Okay, we're done," Dr. Brady announces. "Both of your tubes were open. You're fine."

I look at his screen. I see the two black hair-like tubes. I am sad to leave this place. I feel so good. Maybe this is how Lou Reed felt?

I look down. There's blood on my paper gown.

I look up. Mike is there.

He holds my arm as I stumble back to my locker. The nurse tells me to sit for ten minutes before leaving. Mike hands me the banana pudding, and I eat it in the waiting room. As the high wears off, I think about the fact that my tubes have been open this whole time, and how annoying it is I had to do this test not once but twice to confirm that there was never a problem in the first place.

But there is a problem. Because the tubes are not broken, there is one more thing not to fix. But I'm still not getting pregnant.

I continue not to get pregnant through April, May, and June. I keep taking pills and getting once-a-month shots in my stomach, but nothing is happening. Much has already been written about the negative effect of Trying on your sex life, and I have very little to add except to say it is true. Before we started I had a fantasy that we would be different, that we would continue to have fun and romantic sex, but that notion was as immature as the one I had in junior high school, right when my hormones started raging, that being a prostitute must be super fun, because of all the sex they get to have! Having sex at a specific moment, as an assignment, is a drag. I wonder if there is a personality difference between people conceived spontaneously during hot, condomless one-night stands in Brazil, and people conceived by anxious married couples who schedule medically necessary intercourse in the brief pause between Netflix episodes.

By August, I need a break. I don't want to keep getting blood tests and taking pills and knowing when I'm ovulating. We go on vacation to Martha's Vineyard where I drink tons of wine and eat oysters and relax. We have sex if and when we feel like it.

This is the point in the story that well-meaning people tell couples who are Trying about how, once you stop worrying and just relax, you'll get pregnant. Please do not tell it to anyone you know. It's really annoying and also it's bullshit. I did not get pregnant in August. Or in September, when I also took the month off from Trying.

In October, I report back to Dr. Mukherjee. "Welp," he says. "It might be time to bring in some bigger guns." He thinks I should start doing hormone injections at home. This is the moment I have been fearing, the moment when I transition from Trying 101 to AP Trying. *There is one Hail Mary left*, I think.

I ask Mukherjee if he thinks we could maybe just try one cycle with an IUI.

He shrugs. "Sure, why not," he says, in the same tone he might use if someone asked him if he was interested in a pair of free movie tickets. While Mike and I are in his office we schedule a date in early October to begin. Mukherjee tells us how we will prepare for the procedure, which is supposedly painless. I have to take my pills as usual and come in for my Ovidrel injection and my ultrasound the day before. Mike's only instruction is that for the twenty-four hours before the IUI, in order for his sperm to be at peak numbers when he "donates," he should abstain from masturbating.

A few weeks later, it is the morning of the procedure. I have a terrible cold. In addition to Trying, we are in the process of moving and I have three Airbnb apartments to go see later in the day. I couldn't be more stressed. Then, in the cab on the way to the doctor's office, Mike confesses to me that he forgot his one instruction and masturbated the night before.

On the doctor's table, before I get basted, the nurse shows me the tube of sperm with Mike's name on it. "Confirm this is your husband," she says. There has just been a highly publicized lawsuit against a sperm donor clinic by a lesbian who was basted with the sperm of a black man rather than the white man whose profile she had chosen. I confirm that this is indeed my husband's sperm, but can't help but think for a moment that perhaps some random dark-skinned stranger would have at least had the wherewithal not to jerk it right before the test.

I get basted with my husband's sperm.

Two weeks later, I take a home pregnancy test while Mike is at work. I'm so used to seeing the words NOT PREGNANT appear in the pee stick's window that I know their shape. Still, I stare for a long time at the test.

I'm pregnant.

Fuck you, Dr. Bander.

Six weeks later, we go back to Mukherjee's office for him to perform the ultrasound that will confirm there is indeed an embryo. He is going to check if there is a heartbeat.

Mukherjee himself comes into the room. Up till now, all the ultrasounds have been performed by a nurse. But this is obviously his big moment. He flicks a switch. A ghostly little white thing appears on the screen. He flicks another switch and now we can hear it. *Baboom baboom baboom.*

He presses a button and the machine prints out a picture. "Grain of rice," he says casually. He hands it to us. The first photo. He saunters out of the room.

We clutch this photo, like millions and millions of couples all over the world have done before us. This little piece of shiny black paper with an abstract representation of a thing that is the nexus of thousands of people who used to exist, and don't anymore. My grandparents, our great-great-grandparents, Mike's great-great-great-grandparents. Jews on boats, Jews who didn't make it onto the boats, those pale serious sepia people who always look like ghosts in their formal brown gowns. All of these people forming a chain that goes back to the end of forever, to whatever Jews used to be when they were still amoebas in the ocean like everyone else. For the next three months I pray that all of these ancestors magically pass along their strength to the grain of rice, so he can continue to hang on tight to his little branch of the family tree.

We clutch our piece of paper all the way home. It's printed from a machine my great-great-grandmother could never have even imagined, even though the echo of her molecules is now pulsing through its wires, until they stain this piece of paper with the image of a future boy.

And as I write these words, he is five months old and in the other room. He is a happy baby but is having trouble sleeping. Mike thinks it's time to let him cry it out a bit. I'm not sure. I call him The Champ because he always comes through. He's such a good kid. I know he wants to sleep.

He's Trying.

Acknowledgments

It's so exciting to be writing the acknowledgments for this book. First of all because it means the book is finished, and secondly because there are so many people I want to thank for their generous help in getting me from the first page to the last.

Giant thank-you to Jimmy Miller for believing, early on in my career, that I should be writing stuff at all. Emotional thank-you to David Kuhn and Becky Sweren for making me believe specifically that I both could and should write a book.

Eternal thanks to Emily Griffin for her steadfast confidence in this project and for championing the proposal before it even existed, and to Gretchen Young for taking the baton and getting me across the finish line. A confetti of thanks to everyone at Grand Central Publishing for being just lovely all around, and especially to the eternally kind and patient leader Jamie Raab.

There are a few ladies in particular who have given me more support and encouragement (book-related and otherwise) than I can ever properly thank them for: Kate Grodd, Rebecca Kutys, Maura Madden, and Zubeida Ullah. I love each of you tons.

Michael Lasker, Christie Smith, Tim Phillips, and Ali Waller all were the best of good sports about reading chapter after chapter and telling me to keep going when I really needed to hear someone say to keep going. Bless you all.

In the middle of writing this book, I got preggo and gave birth to my baby boy. It is very hard to write and take care of a baby at the same time, so I owe massive thanks to Bella Luz Antonelli and Lucy Sibrian for taking such incredible care of my son while I was working on this thing.

To the staff of One Girl Cookie in Dumbo, Brooklyn, where a large portion of this book was written: Thank you for letting me sit for hours with my laptop in your establishment and for not saying anything about the fact that I was ordering wine and cake at two in the afternoon.

Thank you to my brother and sister for being Kleins with me and for putting up with a sibling who writes.

Michael: Thank you for being the best and happiest story of my life, and for reminding me, always always always, that more heart is the way to go.

And to the Roo: Thank you for being the sweetest, greatest Roo in the whole world.

Lastly:

My parents spent countless hours teaching me to read and write. My mother was an English teacher who patiently taught me where to put my periods and commas, and my father, who loves books more than anyone I know, taught me from an early age that books are precious and should be handled gently, "like butterflies."

This butterfly exists because of, and for, them.

About the Author

Jessi Klein is the Emmy- and Peabody Award–winning head writer and an executive producer of Comedy Central's critically acclaimed series *Inside Amy Schumer*. She's also written for Amazon's *Transparent* as well as *Saturday Night Live*. She has been featured on the popular storytelling series *The Moth*, and has been a regular panelist on NPR's *Wait Wait…Don't Tell Me!* She's been published in *Esquire* and *Cosmopolitan*, and has had her own half-hour Comedy Central stand-up special.